"Fresh contributions to the longstanding debate over divorce and remarriage are rare. The relevant biblical texts have been picked over for centuries, and the lines of debate have hardened. And yet, somehow, Wayne Grudem has given us that rare, fresh insight into the Bible that changes everything. Grudem affirms the traditional Erasmian view, which allows for divorce and remarriage in cases of sexual immorality and desertion. But he also shows—based on new research on 1 Corinthians 7:15—that divorce and remarriage are permitted in cases of abuse as well. Grudem offers compassionate, biblical advice to those wrestling with the ethics of divorce. Anyone who wishes to understand what the Bible teaches about divorce and remarriage must reckon with this book."

Denny Burk, President, The Council on Biblical Manhood and Womanhood; Professor of Biblical Studies, The Southern Baptist Theological Seminary

"Future generations will thank God for Wayne Grudem's groundbreaking research on the text of 1 Corinthians 7:15 and his broad pastoral wisdom on the Bible's teaching on divorce and remarriage."

R. Kent Hughes, Senior Pastor Emeritus, College Church, Wheaton, Illinois

What the Bible Says about Divorce and Remarriage

Books in This Series

What the Bible Says about Divorce and Remarriage

Wayne Grudem

WHEATON, ILLINOIS

Portions of this book have been adapted from "Divorce and Remarriage" in Wayne Grudem, *Christian Ethics: A Guide to Biblical Moral Reasoning* (Wheaton, IL: Crossway: 2018), 799–842 (chap. 32).

Cover design: Jeff Miller, Faceout Studios

Cover image: Shutterstock

First printing, 2021

Printed in the United States of America

Trade paperback ISBN: 978-1-4335-6826-8
ePub ISBN: 978-1-4335-6829-9
PDF ISBN: 978-1-4335-6827-5
Mobipocket ISBN: 978-1-4335-6828-2

Library of Congress Cataloging-in-Publication Data

Names: Grudem, Wayne A., author.
Title: What the Bible says about divorce and remarriage / Wayne Grudem.
Description: Wheaton, Illinois: Crossway, 2021. | Includes bibliographical references and
   index.
Identifiers: LCCN 2020014733 (print) | LCCN 2020014734 (ebook) | ISBN 9781433568268
   (trade paperback) | ISBN 9781433568275 (pdf) | ISBN 9781433568282 (mobi) |
   ISBN 9781433568299 (epub) Subjects: LCSH: Divorce—Biblical teaching. |
   Remarriage—Biblical
teaching. | Divorce—Religious aspects—Christianity. | Remarriage—Religious
   aspect—Christianity.
Classification: LCC BS680.D62 G78 2021 (print) | LCC BS680.D62 (ebook) | DDC
   261.8/3589—dc23
LC record available at https://lccn.loc.gov/2020014733
LC ebook record available at https://lccn.loc.gov/2020014734

Crossway is a publishing ministry of Good News Publishers.

BP   29   28   27   26   25   24   23   22   21
14   13   12   11   10   9   8   7   6   5   4   3   2   1

Contents

INTRODUCTION

*According to the Bible, what are the legitimate grounds
for divorce, if any?*

*Is divorce morally acceptable in a case of physical abuse
or neglect?*

*If a divorce is granted for biblically legitimate reasons, is
remarriage always allowed?*

Can a divorced person become a church officer?

What reasons are given for the "no remarriage" view?

In marriage, a man and woman commit to live with each other
as husband and wife for life. In order for them to keep this
commitment, *both parties* have to remain in the marriage. But
when one party decides to leave the marriage, either to be with
another partner or simply to end the existing relationship,
it becomes impossible for the remaining spouse to faithfully
fulfill his or her commitment (a husband, for example, cannot *live with* and *act as a husband to* a wife who is living with
another man). Therefore, the question of divorce arises.[1]

---

1. Some portions of this book were adapted from the essay "Divorce and Remarriage" in the *ESV Study Bible* (Wheaton, IL: Crossway, 2008), 2545–47, with
permission of the publisher. (I was the primary author of this article.)

Under what circumstances, if any, is it morally right to obtain a divorce and thereby dissolve a marriage? And if divorce occurs, is it morally right for a divorced person to marry someone else? These and other questions will be addressed in this book.

A. DIVORCE AND ITS CONSEQUENCES

1. The Divorce Rate Is Higher, but Not As High As Is Sometimes Said.

Divorce has now become more common than it was in previous generations. In the early part of the twentieth century, the divorce rate in the United States was approximately 0.9 per 1,000 total population.[2] Throughout the twentieth century the divorce rate slowly increased, then rose rapidly in the 1970s and 1980s as many states passed no-fault divorce laws.[3] The divorce rate peaked in the early 1980s at approximately 5.0 per 1,000 total population (approximately 1.2 million divorces).[4] After 1985, the divorce rate gradually declined, so that in 2018 there were approximately 782,038 divorces or annulments in America, or 2.9 per 1,000 total population.[5] But the

---

2. "Marriages and Divorces, 1900–2012," Information Please, citing information from the U.S. Centers for Disease Control and Prevention, National Center for Health Statistics, http://www.infoplease.com/ipa /A0005044.html.

3. No-fault divorce laws allow for a divorce to be granted without any requirement to show that one party to the marriage has committed some wrongdoing (such as adultery, desertion, or cruelty) that makes the marriage unworkable. In a no-fault divorce proceeding, one of the parties simply has to show that the marriage is no longer viable and is beyond repair (for example, because of "irreconcilable differences") without having to prove that the other party is responsible. Specific requirements vary from state to state.

4. "Marriages and Divorces, 1900–2012."

5. Centers for Disease Control and Prevention, National Center for Health Statistics, National Marriage and Divorce Trends, https://www.cdc.gov/nchs/nvss

number of divorces per 1,000 population has gone down primarily because many couples are now living together instead of getting married and more people are remaining single. (There were approximately 10.6 marriages per 1,000 people in the early 1980s, but only 6.8 marriages per 1,000 people in 2009–2013 and 6.5 per 1,000 people in 2018.[6])

However, it is not true that 50 percent of marriages end in divorce today (a statistic that is sometimes repeated in popular media reports). After extensive statistical analysis, social researcher Shaunti Feldhahn reported in 2014, "According to one of the most recent Census Bureau surveys, 72 percent of people who have ever been married are still married to their first spouse"—and the remaining 28 percent are not all divorced persons, because the total also includes those who have been widowed through the death of a spouse, a category that accounts for perhaps as many as 8 percent.[7] That suggests that "somewhere around 20 to 25 percent of first marriages end in divorce."[8] Feldhahn concludes, "Imagine the difference to our collective consciousness if we say 'Most marriages last a lifetime' rather than 'Half of marriages end in divorce.'"[9]

/marriage_divorce_tables.htm. "National Marriage and Divorce Rate Trends," table linked at https://www.cdc.gov/nchs/fastats/marriage-divorce.htm. Note: The CDC's statistics exclude data for California, Georgia, Hawaii, Indiana, and Minnesota.

6. "National Marriage and Divorce Rate Trends."

7. Shaunti Feldhahn, *The Good News about Marriage: Debunking Discouraging Myths about Marriage and Divorce* (Colorado Springs: Multnomah, 2014), 21–22.

8. Feldhahn, *The Good News about Marriage*, 22.

9. Feldhahn, *The Good News about Marriage*, 25.

The divorce rate is even lower for those who attend church regularly. Feldhahn says:

> Weekly church attendance alone lowers the divorce rate significantly—roughly 25 to 50 percent, depending on the study. The popular belief that the rate of divorce is the same inside and outside the church is based on a deeply entrenched *misunderstanding* about the results of several George Barna surveys over the past decades. A misunderstanding that, Mr. Barna told me, he would love to correct in the public's mind.[10]

Speaking personally, I have long been skeptical of the claims that 50 percent of marriages end in divorce and that the divorce rate among evangelical Christians is the same as in the general society. I have been skeptical because such claims seemed to be wildly inaccurate in terms of the people we have known. Margaret and I have come to know many hundreds and probably thousands of actual married couples over our 51 years of marriage. We have lived in six different states and two countries (we spent over four years in the UK); we have been active members of nine different churches; and I have taught for 43 years in three different educational institutions with hundreds of students, and the number of divorces that we are aware of is absolutely tiny, certainly less than 5 percent of the married couples we have known and probably closer to 1 percent.

---

10. Feldhahn, *The Good News about Marriage*, 66.

Marriage counselors Jan and David Stoop report similar anecdotal evidence:

> One couple, who work together in a marriage ministry involving many couples, shared in their response to our questionnaire that they had found only one couple in 1500 who pray together on a regular basis ever gets divorced.[11]

Feldhahn includes other encouraging statistics about marriage, tabulating sociological research from multiple sources. She reports, "The median number of those who say they are in happy marriages is around 90 percent," and, after discounting for some statistical variability, she concludes, "The actual percentage of happy marriages could be a bit lower or higher, but 80 percent seems like a very safe—in some ways, even conservative—number."[12]

However, it is still the case that millions of couples in the United States and other countries, including Christian couples, get divorced every year. And therefore it is important that we understand the teaching of God's Word on this issue, and that we understand more fully the consequences of divorce as well.

2. The Tragic Consequences of Divorce. Because divorce is more common today than in previous generations, some people might assume that it is less harmful in people's lives

---

11. Jan Stoop and David Stoop, *When Couples Pray Together: Creating Intimacy and Spiritual Wholeness* (Ann Arbor, MI: Servant, 2000), 31.

12. Feldhahn, *The Good News about Marriage*, 66.

than it used to be. But the most thorough long-term study of the consequences of divorce does not confirm that assumption. The study was headed by Judith Wallerstein, founder and executive director of the Center for the Family in Transition in Corte Madera, California. The results of this study have been published in a number of books stretching over many years.[13]

The results of Wallerstein's study are heartbreaking, and I can only mention a few points. She and her colleagues interviewed 60 families (120 parents with 131 children) who were going through divorces in 1971. They then interviewed the same people at intervals of one year, five years, and 10 years after the divorces in order to ascertain the results on people's lives. No other study of this magnitude has ever been done on the long-term consequences of divorce.[14]

Here are some of the notable conclusions from the study:

Men and women tell us very clearly at the 10-year mark that the stress of being a single parent never lightens

---

13. The material that I cite below is taken from the study published 10 years after divorces had occurred: Judith Wallerstein and Sandra Blakeslee, *Second Chances: Men, Women, and Children a Decade after Divorce* (New York: Ticknor and Fields, 1989). Supplemental material that does not contradict but largely affirms the earlier study is found in Judith Wallerstein, Julia Lewis, and Sandra Blakeslee, *The Unexpected Legacy of Divorce: The 25 Year Landmark Study* (New York: Hyperion, 2000).

14. Wallerstein explains that the researchers chose a homogeneous population group for their study, in which the majority of the men were highly educated professionals or were owners of or in management positions in businesses, and 75 percent of the women had at least some college education. Half of the families belonged to churches or synagogues. Wallerstein says, "This, then, is divorce under the best of circumstances." Wallerstein and Blakeslee, *Second Chances*, xv.

and that the fear of being alone never ceases. (*Second Chances*, p. 10)

Incredibly, one-half of the women and one-third of the men are still intensely angry at their former spouses despite the passage of 10 years. Because their feelings have not changed, anger has become an ongoing, and sometimes dominant, presence in their children's lives as well. (p. 29)

In only one in seven of the former couples did the former wife and husband experience stable second marriages. (p. 41)

Some men and women seem to be held together by marriage; it brings order and security to their lives, and the structure itself provides their *raison d'être* and their highest level of adult adjustment. For both men and women, marriage in middle or later life has an additional and very important function: it provides an internal buffer against the anxieties of aging, of being old and alone, and of facing the inevitability of death. It also provides external supports to cope with the increasing disabilities and infirmities of old age. When the structure is removed, they are left feeling extremely vulnerable, and the external symptoms of physical deterioration are symbolic of the internal conflict and emotional distress. (p. 53)

People like to think that because there are so many divorced families, adults and children will find divorce easier or even easy. But neither parents nor children find comfort in numbers. Divorce is not a more "normal" experience simply because so many people have been touched by it. Our findings revealed that all children suffer from divorce, no matter how many of their friends have gone through it. . . . Each and every child cries out, "Why me?" (p. 303)

Children of all ages feel intensely rejected when their parents divorce. . . . Some keep their anger hidden for years out of fear of upsetting parents or for fear of retribution and punishment; others show it. (p. 12)

Children feel intense loneliness. . . . Even when children are encouraged not to take sides, they often feel that they must. However, when they do take sides to feel more protected, they also feel despair because they are betraying one parent over the other. If they do not take sides, they feel isolated and disloyal to both parents. There is no solution to their dilemma. (p. 13)

[After 10 and sometimes 15 years,] even though they no longer have any illusions that their parents could ever remarry their sense of loss and wistful yearning persists, and their emotions run deep and strong. They feel less protected, less cared for, less comforted. . . . These children share vivid, gut-wrenching memories of their parents' separation. (p. 23)

[Nearly one-third of the children] between the ages of 19 and 29 have little or no ambition 10 years after their parents' divorce. They are drifting through life with no set goals, limited educations, and a sense of helplessness. . . . They don't make long-term plans and are aiming below the intellectual and educational achievements of their fathers and mothers. (pp. 148–49)

One of the great tragedies of divorce is that many fathers have absolutely no idea that their children feel rejected. . . . Without the continued support of their fathers, these boys lack self-confidence and pride in their own masculinity. . . . [The girls] too feel hurt, unsure of their femininity, and insecure in their relationships with men. . . . Many young people, especially boys, cannot express the anger they feel toward the parent who is rejecting them. (pp. 150–51)

I am not quoting this material to say that such destructive consequences are inevitable, for statistics and probabilities do not imply certain results for any one individual. In addition, Christians who go through divorce and Christians who provide support to those going through divorce have the additional factor of the power of the Holy Spirit to heal people's lives. Sometimes long-standing anger or fear can be changed by the Holy Spirit's transforming power working within people in answer to prayer. And well-functioning churches can often provide the effective "family" that will make up in some measure for what is lost in divorce. Still, these sobering findings help us understand why God established a wonderful moral standard of lifelong marriage between one man and one woman as the pattern for marriages in the human race (see the next section).

One verse that is commonly understood to reveal God's own sorrow regarding the painful consequences of divorce is found in the last book of the Old Testament. According to several translations, Malachi says this:

> "For I hate divorce," says the LORD, the God of Israel, "and him who covers his garment with wrong," says the LORD of hosts. (Mal. 2:16 NASB)[15]

If this is the correct translation, it does not mean that God considers all divorces to be morally wrong (for other passages of Scripture must be considered), but only that God is deeply grieved to see the painful consequences that flow from divorces.

Whatever view one takes of Malachi 2:16, interpreters who have differing views of this verse still agree that the consistent emphasis of both the Old and New Testaments is on the importance of preserving marriage and avoiding divorce in all but a few very narrowly defined circumstances.

B. GOD'S ORIGINAL PLAN IS FOR LIFELONG MONOGAMOUS MARRIAGE

God's original plan for the human race, as indicated in his creation of Adam and Eve as husband and wife (Gen.

---

15. The RSV, NRSV, NET, NIV 1984, and NLT all translate this as God saying, "I hate divorce." The ESV translates this sentence as "For the man who does not love his wife but divorces her, says the LORD, the God of Israel, covers his garment with violence, says the LORD of hosts." See the appendix (p. 88) for a discussion of the translation issues involved in this difficult verse.

1:27–28; 2:22–25), is lifelong, monogamous marriage. Jesus affirmed this in responding to a question about divorce:

> And Pharisees came up to him and tested him by asking, "Is it lawful to divorce one's wife for any cause?" He answered, "Have you not read that he who created them from the beginning made them male and female [from Gen. 1:27], and said, 'Therefore a man shall leave his father and his mother and hold fast to his wife, and the two shall become one flesh' [from Gen. 2:24]? So they are no longer two but one flesh. *What therefore God has joined together, let not man separate.*" (Matt. 19:3–6)

In this reply Jesus rebukes and corrects a first-century practice of easy divorce for trivial reasons. For example, the Mishnah said:

> The school of Shammai say: A man may not divorce his wife unless he has found unchastity in her. . . . And the school of Hillel say . . . [he may divorce her] even if she spoiled a dish for him. . . . Rabbi Akiba says, [he may divorce her] even if he found another fairer than she. (Mishnah, *Gittin* 9:10)[16]

Rather than entering into this debate among rabbis, Jesus affirms God's original plan for marriage and shows that it is still his ideal for all marriages.

---

16. The Mishnah was put in written form in the late second century or early third century AD, but it reflects earlier oral tradition, including much from before the time of Christ. With respect to this particular quotation, both Hillel (died AD 10) and Shammai (50 BC–AD 30) lived prior to Jesus's earthly ministry.

The Old Testament prophet Malachi views marriage as a "covenant" between a husband and wife. Furthermore, God is a witness to this covenant, and he will hold people accountable for it: "The Lord was witness between you and the wife of your youth, to whom you have been faithless, *though she is your companion and your wife by covenant*" (Mal. 2:14). Therefore, marriage is an especially serious commitment (1) between husband and wife, (2) to the society in which they live, and (3) before God himself (whether or not he is explicitly acknowledged in the marriage ceremony).

It is important to begin this book about divorce and remarriage with a clear affirmation that God's original intention is that a husband and wife remain married to each other for their entire lives, or, as the traditional marriage ceremony puts it, "so long as you both shall live." Although the following discussion will show that God allowed divorce as a remedy in some cases where marriages were irreparably damaged, Scripture still shows that God's ideal is lifelong, monogamous marriage, and that the first question to be asked of any couple contemplating divorce should be, "Is it possible that this marriage can be restored and preserved?"

C. IN THE OLD TESTAMENT, DIVORCE WAS ALLOWED IN CERTAIN CASES

The only Old Testament law concerning divorce is found in Deuteronomy 24:

When a man takes a wife and marries her, if then she finds no favor in his eyes because he has found some indecency in her, *and he writes her a certificate of divorce* and puts it in her hand and sends her out of his house, and she departs out of his house, *and if she goes and becomes another man's wife*, and the latter man hates her and writes her a certificate of divorce and puts it in her hand and sends her out of his house, or if the latter man dies, who took her to be his wife, then *her former husband, who sent her away, may not take her again to be his wife*, after she has been defiled, for that is an abomination before the LORD. And you shall not bring sin upon the land that the LORD your God is giving you for an inheritance. (vv. 1–4)

This is not the kind of law that says something like "A person may obtain a divorce for such-and-such a reason." There is no law exactly like that anywhere in the Old Testament. Rather, this passage *assumes* that some divorces would take place between a husband and wife "because he has found some indecency in her" (v. 1), but the text does not specify exactly what that "indecency" is.[17] This text only specifies that a woman may not return to her first husband in the following circumstance:

---

17. Other translations speak of "some indecency" (NASB, RSV), "something indecent" (NIV, CSB), "something offensive" (NET), "something improper" (HCSB), or "some uncleanness" (KJV, NKJV). The Hebrew expression *'erwat dābār*, "the nakedness/shamefulness of a thing," is quite vague, and John Murray wisely says, "It is exceedingly difficult if not precarious to be certain as to what the 'unseemly thing' really was." *Divorce* (Philadelphia: Presbyterian and Reformed, 1961), 9.

1. if he divorces her because he finds "some indecency" in her, *and*
2. if she marries another man, *and*
3. if that second husband dies or divorces her;
4. then her first husband may not remarry her.

We can notice, however, that the passage assumes that, after the divorce, the woman had a right to marry some-one else, and that second marriage was not considered to be adultery but to be a legitimate marriage: She "becomes another man's wife" (Deut. 24:2).[18]

Other passages in the Old Testament also assume that divorces were occurring among the Jewish people, indi-cating that, even if God did not command divorce in any specific circumstances, he tolerated it and to some degree regulated it, at least in some cases:

> They [the priests] shall not marry a prostitute or a
> woman who has been defiled, neither shall they marry
> a woman divorced from her husband, for the priest
> is holy to his God. (Lev. 21:7; the verse assumes that
> those who were not priests could marry "a woman
> divorced from her husband")[19]

> But if a priest's daughter is widowed or divorced and
> has no child and returns to her father's house, as in her
> youth, she may eat of her father's food. (Lev. 22:13)

---

18. Murray writes, "One thing is certain, that the second marriage was not placed in the category of adultery. . . . The woman and her second husband were not put to death as the Pentateuch required in the case of adultery." Murray, *Divorce*, 14–15.

19. See a similar restriction in Ezek. 44:22.

But any vow of a widow or of a divorced woman, anything by which she has bound herself, shall stand against her. (Num. 30:9)

[If a man accuses his wife of not being a virgin when they got married, and if her parents bring proof of her virginity to the elders, then] he may not divorce her all his days. (Deut. 22:19; the verse assumes that divorce was a possibility in other marriages; see also v. 29)

She saw that for all the adulteries of that faithless one, Israel, I had sent her away with a decree of divorce. Yet her treacherous sister Judah did not fear, but she too went and played the whore. (Jer. 3:8; in this verse, God portrays himself as a husband who "sent away"—that is, divorced—his unfaithful wife because of all her "adulteries"—that is, her worship of other gods)

But these Old Testament passages do not give us much guidance regarding ethical standards for divorce in the new covenant age because (1) they assume that divorces would occur without giving us specific details about how to know when divorce is morally justified and (2) they all belong to the Mosaic covenant, which is no longer in effect in the new covenant age in which we now live.[20]

---

20. See the discussion about the end of the Mosaic covenant in Wayne Grudem, *Christian Ethics: An Introduction to Biblical Moral Reasoning* (Wheaton, IL: Crossway, 2018), 209–63 (chap. 8).

D. IN THE NEW TESTAMENT, DIVORCE IS EXPLICITLY ALLOWED IN TWO CASES

Christian interpreters have held different views about divorce and remarriage for several centuries, and every scriptural passage about divorce has been extensively debated among commentators. In this section I will give an overview of my understanding of the relevant New Testament passages, and then later in the book I will interact with alternative interpretations.

1. Jesus Allowed for Divorce and Remarriage on Account of Adultery.

a. Matthew 19:3–9: We can now examine in more detail Matthew 19:3–9, which (along with its parallel in Mark 10:2–12) is the longest passage in the Bible dealing with the topic of divorce. I will discuss this longer passage first and then examine Matthew 5:32, which is the shorter passage about divorce in Matthew. As we will see, Jesus was establishing a far stricter requirement regarding divorce than the standard taught by many rabbis of his day.

Earlier in this book, I quoted the first four verses of Matthew 19:3–9, but here is the passage in its entirety:

> And Pharisees came up to him and tested him by asking, "Is it lawful to divorce one's wife for any cause?" He answered, "Have you not read that he who created them from the beginning made them male and fe-

male, and said, 'Therefore a man shall leave his father and his mother and hold fast to his wife, and the two shall become one flesh'? So they are no longer two but one flesh. What therefore God has joined together, let not man separate." They said to him, "Why then did Moses command one to give a certificate of divorce and to send her away?" He said to them, "*Because of your hardness of heart Moses allowed you to divorce your wives, but from the beginning it was not so. And I say to you: whoever divorces his wife, except for sexual immorality, and marries another, commits adultery.*"

Jesus's statement "Because of your hardness of heart . . ." should not be understood to mean that only "hard-hearted" people *initiate* divorces, but rather, "because your hard-hearted rebellion against God led to serious defilement of marriages." The presence of sin in the community meant that some marriages would be deeply harmed by hard-hearted spouses, and therefore Moses "allowed" the *other* spouse to obtain a divorce. God was providing a partial remedy for the harm that a hard-hearted husband or wife could do to the other person in the marriage.

In the final verse of this passage, Jesus provides significant guidance about divorce in the new covenant age:

And I say to you: whoever divorces his wife, except for sexual immorality, *and marries another*, commits adultery. (Matt. 19:9)

The first thing to notice is that Jesus decisively terminates all other grounds by which people were divorcing their wives because of liberal Jewish interpretations of Deuteronomy 24:1–4. The only legitimate reason to initiate a divorce is "sexual immorality" committed by one's spouse. Jesus is certainly not approving easy divorces. According to this passage, he is prohibiting divorces for reasons other than adultery. He is directly contradicting the viewpoints promoted by followers of the rabbinic school of Hillel and the followers of Akiba, because "the school of Hillel say . . . [he may divorce her] even if she spoiled a dish for him. . . . Rabbi Akiba says, [he may divorce her] even if he found another fairer than she" (Mishnah, *Gittin* 9:10).

The implication of Jesus's statement is that divorce for reasons other than adultery does not actually dissolve a marriage in the eyes of God. This is clear because Jesus says that a man who divorces his wife "except for sexual immorality, and marries another, *commits adultery*" (Matt. 19:9). But "adultery" (Greek, *moichaomai*) can only be committed by a married person. This means that Jesus is saying that a man who wrongly divorces his wife has not received a legitimate divorce and is in fact still married to his original wife at the time he initiates the second marriage.[21]

Jesus's disciples apparently were shocked at the strictness of his teaching in comparison to that of many of the rabbis of that day, for they said to him in the following

---

21. If marriage is a solemn covenant made in the presence of God (see Grudem, *Christian Ethics*, 701), then God's decision about whether a husband and wife are still married or not is highly significant.

verse, "If such is the case of a man with his wife, it is better not to marry" (Matt. 19:10). They jumped to the conclusion that it would be safer never to get married than to be stuck in an unhappy marriage for one's whole life. But Jesus corrected their misunderstanding, explaining that the calling and the ability not to be married was itself something that was only "given" by God to certain people. The conversation went like this:

> The disciples said to him, "If such is the case of a man with his wife, it is better not to marry." But he said to them, "Not everyone can receive this saying [that is, the saying that "it is better not to marry"], *but only those to whom it is given.* For there are eunuchs who have been so from birth, and there are eunuchs who have been made eunuchs by men, and there are eunuchs who have made themselves eunuchs for the sake of the kingdom of heaven. Let the one who is able to receive this receive it." (Matt. 19:10–12)

But when Jesus allowed *divorce* because of adultery, this was also a break with the Old Testament law, under which the penalty for adultery was death (see Lev. 20:10; Deut. 22:22; cf. John 8:4–5). Although it is unlikely that first-century Jewish people, living under the Roman government more than 1,400 years after the time of Moses, were actually carrying out the death penalty for adultery,[22] the law

---

22. The Roman Empire did not allow anyone except its own officials to carry out the death penalty. This is why the Jewish accusers of Jesus said to Pilate, "It is not lawful for us to put anyone to death" (John 18:31). For discussion of the

was still there in Leviticus and Deuteronomy. But in the new covenant age, according to Jesus's teaching, the penalty for adultery would no longer be death but the "sending away" involved in divorce (or perhaps even forgiveness and the restoration of the marriage, for Jesus *allows* divorce for adultery but he does not *command* it).

We must emphasize that when Jesus says that "whoever divorces his wife, *except for sexual immorality*, and marries another, commits adultery" (Matt. 19:9), he implies the converse: divorce and remarriage on the ground of sexual immorality are *not* prohibited and do *not* constitute adultery.

Here is an example of a similar "except for" statement from my work as a seminary professor: Suppose that I say this to my class:

> Whoever hands in a term paper after Tuesday at 9 a.m., *except for students who have received a deadline extension from me*, will receive a reduction of one letter grade per day.

This statement implies that a student who hands in a late paper but has received a deadline extension *will not* receive a reduction of one letter grade per day. In the same way, Jesus's statement "except for sexual immorality" implies that a man who divorces his wife because of sexual immorality and marries another person does *not* commit adultery.

---

extrabiblical historical evidence, see D. A. Carson, *The Gospel According to John*, The Pillar New Testament Commentary (Grand Rapids, MI: Eerdmans, 1991), 591–92.

This statement from Jesus is also significant for the question of remarriage. When Jesus says, "and marries another," he implies that *both divorce and remarriage are allowed* in the case of sexual immorality, and that someone who divorces because his spouse has committed adultery may marry someone else without committing sin. This is evident because if we remove "and marries another," the saying does not make any sense:

> And I say to you: *whoever divorces his wife*, except for sexual immorality, . . . *commits adultery*.

But that would not be true, because some husbands will divorce their wives and then they will not remarry or live with any other woman. They will remain single and chaste. In that case, they would not be committing adultery with anyone, and Jesus's words would not make sense. Therefore, the phrase "and marries another" must be present for the verse to make sense. And that means that "whoever divorces his wife . . . *and marries another*" because of sexual immorality is not committing adultery in that second marriage.

As for the meaning of the exception clause, the expression "sexual immorality" in Jesus's statement translates the Greek term *porneia*, which was a broad term that included all kinds of sexually immoral conduct.[23] It certainly included

---

23. See Walter Bauer et al., *A Greek-English Lexicon of the New Testament and Other Early Christian Literature*, 3rd ed. (Chicago: University of Chicago Press, 2000), 854. See also my further discussion of this term in Grudem, *Christian Ethics*, 720.

adultery,[24] as well as prostitution, incest, homosexuality, and bestiality.[25]

In conclusion, if "sexual immorality" occurs, then Jesus says that divorce is allowed. But he does not say that divorce is required. Even in such cases, forgiveness and reconciliation should always be the first option.

b. Divorce in the First Century Always Included the Right to Remarry: In Greek, Roman, and Jewish cultures in the first century, wherever divorce was allowed, the right to remarry was always assumed to accompany it. Regarding the Jewish culture, the Mishnah says:

> The essential formula in the bill of divorce is, "lo, thou art free to marry any man." (Mishnah, *Gittin* 9:3)[26]

---

24. The term *porneia* is used to refer to adultery in Rev. 17:2 as well as in the Apocrypha (Sir. 23:23) and in the early Christian writing *Shepherd of Hermas* (Mandate 4.1.5).

25. But *porneia* would *not* include, in ordinary usage, committing "adultery" in one's heart by looking at a woman with lustful intent, as someone might wish to argue from Matt. 5:28, any more than becoming angry with someone would mean that you have "murdered" the person according to Matt. 5:21–22 and you should be subject to capital punishment! In ordinary Greek usage, *porneia* referred only to physical actions of sexual immorality, and Jesus recognized that, because he had to add "in his heart" to show that he was speaking about a different kind of adultery, not the physical act, in Matt. 5:28.

I should add, however, that it seems to me possible that the kinds of sexual sin implied by the term *porneia* could also include, in today's world, such extensive sexual defilement of a marriage as is committed by a husband who repeatedly visits strip clubs or indulges an ongoing addiction to pornography. Each situation is different, and if such an actual situation comes up involving someone in a church, my recommendation would be that the church elder board should accept the difficult responsibility of evaluating the case and seeking to make a wise decision.

26. David Instone-Brewer says the divorce formula that said, "You are allowed to marry any man you wish" (or close equivalent), can be traced as far back as the fifth century BC in Jewish documents, and as far back as the 14th century BC in Babylonian marriage certificates and law codes. *Divorce and Remarriage in the Bible: The Social and Literary Context* (Grand Rapids, MI: Eerdmans, 2002), 29.

In Greek culture, "a man could divorce his wife by sending her back to her father, who could then give her in marriage to a second husband."[27] And in Roman culture, "Although the virtue and good fortune of a woman who in her lifetime had only one husband was valued . . . , remarriage was acceptable and necessary."[28]

This does not necessarily mean that Jesus had to agree with any of the surrounding cultures on this issue, but it does mean that if Jesus intended to teach that divorce was sometimes allowed but remarriage was never allowed, he would have had to make it exceptionally clear in his teaching. Otherwise his hearers, as well as readers of the Gospels throughout the Roman Empire, would naturally have assumed that where divorce is allowed, the right to remarry someone else is also allowed.

c. Matthew 5:32: In this verse, Jesus affirms essentially the same teaching as in Matthew 19:

> But I say to you that everyone who divorces his wife, *except on the ground of sexual immorality*, makes her commit adultery, and whoever marries a divorced woman commits adultery.

Jesus says that the husband who wrongfully divorces his wife "makes her commit adultery." In that society it was assumed that a divorced woman would need to marry

---

27. "Marriage Law," in *Oxford Classical Dictionary*, 3rd ed., ed. Simon Hornblower and Antony Spawforth (Oxford: Oxford University Press, 1996), 928.
28. "Marriage Law," in *Oxford Classical Dictionary*, 928.

someone else for financial support and protection, and yet Jesus still says this new marriage begins with "adultery" because there was not a proper reason for her divorce (sexual immorality). But Jesus places most of the blame on the original husband who wrongly divorced her, saying that he thereby "makes her commit adultery."[29]

The exception that we saw in Matthew 19 is also present in this passage: "except on the ground of sexual immorality." Here again, Jesus is teaching that divorce is allowed in the case of sexual immorality. He is simply teaching that divorce for other, less serious reasons, is not acceptable.

In the last sentence of the passage, "whoever marries a divorced woman" should be taken together with the preceding words in this sentence. Understood in this context, this last clause does not directly contradict the previous part of the verse (and Matt. 19:9), where Jesus allows the legitimacy of divorce because of adultery. Rather, this clause is continuing

---

29. An alternative translation is, "anyone who divorces his wife, except for sexual immorality, *makes her the victim of adultery*" (Matt. 5:32 NIV). However, I found no other English version that translates it this way, and such a translation does not seem necessary. The Greek verb is *moicheuthēnai*, an aorist passive infinitive of the verb *moicheuō*, for which Bauer et al. give the meaning "to commit adultery," and under that meaning say the passive voice can be used in the case of a woman, as in Sir. 23:23 ("Through her fornication she has *committed adultery* and brought forth children by another man," NRSV); Philo, *On the Decalogue*, 124; Josephus, *Antiquities of the Jews*, 7.131; and John 8:4. Bauer et al., *A Greek-English Lexicon of the New Testament*, 657. In addition, Henry George Liddell, Robert Scott, and Henry Stuart Jones cite Aristotle, *Historia Animalium*, 586.a.3, as another example of a passive form of *moicheuō* used with an active sense to speak of "the woman in Sicily who *committed adultery* (*moicheutheisa*) with the Ethiopian." Liddell-Scott-Jones, *A Greek-English Lexicon*, 9th ed. (Oxford, UK: Clarendon, 1996), 1141. Neither Bauer et al. nor Liddell, Scott, and Jones give "to be the victim of adultery" as a possible meaning for the passive voice of the verb, nor does Franco Montanari, *The Brill Dictionary of Ancient Greek* (Leiden and Boston: Brill, 2015), 1357.

the same topic that he is discussing in the earlier part of the verse, and so it means "and whoever marries *such a wrongly divorced woman as I have just spoken about* . . ."

d. Mark 10:11–12 and Luke 16:18:

> And he said to them, "*Whoever divorces his wife and marries another commits adultery against her*, and if she divorces her husband and marries another, she commits adultery." (Mark 10:11–12)

> *Everyone who divorces his wife and marries another commits adultery*, and he who marries a woman divorced from her husband commits adultery. (Luke 16:18)

In these statements about divorce in Mark and Luke, Jesus does not include the exception clause "except for sexual immorality." The most likely reason is that there was no dispute or disagreement among Jews, or in Greek or Roman culture, that adultery was a legitimate ground for divorce, and Jesus is not addressing that issue. The disputes among the Jews of that time were rather about how many *other* grounds of divorce were legitimate (such as spoiling a meal!).

The primary force of Jesus's statements in these verses is to nullify the practice of divorce for trivial reasons that many Jewish interpreters were defending from Deuteronomy 24. In both Mark and Luke, Jesus decisively nullifies those practices. This does not invalidate the more extensive teaching given in Matthew, because the exception for adultery is assumed but not stated explicitly in Mark and Luke.

It is common in ordinary speech to fail to make pedantic qualifications to a statement when both the speaker and the hearers assume that the qualifications apply and do not need to be stated. For example, suppose a teenage girl in Arizona said to her father, "Dad, can I drive 100 mph on Highway 101?" Her father would probably reply, "No—anybody who drives 100 mph on Highway 101 will be arrested." He does not need to add, "unless you are a policeman in pursuit of a criminal," because everyone assumes that to be true.

Another example is Jesus's statement that "everyone who looks at a woman with lustful intent has already committed adultery with her in his heart" (Matt. 5:28). But there is an unexpressed exception that is assumed: "everyone who looks at a woman *except for his wife*."[30]

Similarly, in a context where there was no controversy about the legitimacy of divorce because of adultery, there was no need to specifically state that exception.

2. Paul Adds Desertion as a Second Reason for Divorce. Paul gives a second legitimate reason for divorce in 1 Corinthians 7:10–15:

> To the married I give this charge (not I, but the Lord): the wife should not separate from her husband (but if she does, she should remain unmarried or else be reconciled to her husband), and the husband should not divorce his wife.

---

30. This exception was pointed out to me by Andy Naselli.

To the rest I say (I, not the Lord) that if any brother has a wife who is an unbeliever, and she consents to live with him, he should not divorce her. If any woman has a husband who is an unbeliever, and he consents to live with her, she should not divorce him. For the unbelieving husband is made holy because of his wife, and the unbelieving wife is made holy because of her husband. Otherwise your children would be unclean, but as it is, they are holy. *But if the unbelieving partner separates, let it be so. In such cases the brother or sister is not enslaved.* God has called you to peace.

In the first two verses (vv. 10–11), Paul teaches that husbands and wives should stay together, and if for some reason they separate for a time, they should not marry someone else, but should seek to be reconciled to each other and come to live together once again.

When Paul says "not I, but the Lord," and then later says, "I, not the Lord," he is distinguishing a matter on which he has a record of Jesus's own teaching about marriage (1 Cor. 7:10–11) from a matter about which Jesus did not leave any specific teaching (vv. 12–15).[31] In churches such as the one in Corinth, Paul was facing a new situation that Jesus had not addressed—that of a Christian and non-Christian married to each other. (In the context in which Jesus was speaking, Jewish people only married other Jews, and both husband and wife therefore were part of the Jewish religious community.)

---

31. See further discussion in Wayne Grudem, *Systematic Theology: An Introduction to Biblical Doctrine* (Leicester, UK: Inter-Varsity, and Grand Rapids, MI: Zondervan, 1994), 76–77.

When a believer has an unbelieving spouse, Paul says that they should remain married if the unbeliever is willing to do so (1 Cor. 7:12–14).[32] Then he adds:

> But *if the unbelieving partner separates, let it be so*. In such cases the brother or sister is not enslaved. God has called you to peace. (1 Cor. 7:15)

The most likely interpretation of this verse is that it implies the freedom to obtain a legal divorce and the freedom to marry someone else. The spouse who has been abandoned "is not enslaved" to the marriage partner. When an unbelieving spouse has deserted the marriage, God releases the believing spouse from the twin unending stresses of (1) a lifelong vain hope of reconciling with an unbeliever who has left and (2) a lifelong prohibition against enjoying the good blessings of marriage again.

Would this passage apply to desertion by someone who professes to be a Christian? In such cases, a question arises as to whether the person is genuinely a believer or has simply made a false profession of faith. Each situation will be different, and a Christian involved in such a difficult circumstance should seek wise counsel from the leaders of

---

32. This direction to remain married to an unbelieving wife or husband stands in contrast to the situation in Ezra 10, in which the exiles who had returned from Babylon to Jerusalem agreed to "put away" (or to "cause to go out"; Hiphil verb stem of *yātsā'*) their foreign wives (Ezra 10:3). However, the *ESV Study Bible* notes that in the statement "We have broken faith with our God and have *married* foreign women from the peoples of the land" (Ezra 10:2), the word translated as "married" (Hiphil of *yāshab*, "to dwell") is not the usual one, but means literally "we have given a home," and that these words "may imply that these illicit relationships were not marriages in the full sense." *ESV Study Bible* (Wheaton, IL: Crossway, 2008), 819.

his or her church. Where possible, the steps of church discipline outlined in Matthew 18:15–17 should be followed in an attempt to bring reconciliation to the marriage. If that process results in the final step of excommunication from the church, then it would seem appropriate to treat the deserting spouse as an unbeliever ("Let him be to you as a Gentile and a tax collector," Matt. 18:17). But it must be emphasized that if reconciliation of the marriage can at all be brought about, that should always be the first goal.

3. At Least Two Legitimate Grounds for Divorce. When we combine the teaching of Jesus with the teaching of Paul on this subject, it seems that there are at least two legitimate grounds for divorce: (1) adultery and (2) desertion by an unbeliever when all reasonable attempts at reconciliation have failed (including desertion by a professing Christian who has refused all the steps of church discipline and has come to be treated as an unbeliever).

The position that I have briefly summarized here—that both divorce and remarriage are allowed when a person's spouse has committed adultery or has irreparably deserted the marriage—is the most common position that has been held among Protestants since the Reformation. This is the position set forth, for example, in the Westminster Confession of Faith (1646):

In the case of adultery after marriage, it is lawful for the innocent party to sue out a divorce: and, after the divorce, to marry another, as if the offending party were dead. . . . Nothing but *adultery*, or such *willful desertion* as can no way be remedied by the church or civil magistrate, is cause sufficient of dissolving the bond of marriage. (24.5, 6, emphasis added)

This is the position defended in the extensive exegetical argument by John Murray[33] and in the careful and detailed but less technical discussions by Jay Adams[34] and Thomas Edgar.[35] It is also the position advocated in ethics texts by John Jefferson Davis,[36] John Feinberg and Paul Feinberg,[37] and Robertson McQuilkin and Paul Copan[38] (see bibliography at the end of this book for details).

E. ARE THERE ANY ADDITIONAL LEGITIMATE GROUNDS FOR DIVORCE?

In addition to the two grounds of sexual immorality and desertion by an unbeliever, are there any other legiti-

---

33. Murray, *Divorce*. This entire book consists of a detailed exegetical study of the biblical passages related to divorce. D. A. Carson also gives an extended defense of the view that, in Matt. 19:3–12, Jesus allows both divorce and remarriage in the case of adultery: see D. A. Carson, "Matthew," in *Matthew & Mark (Revised Edition)*, vol. 9 in the Expositor's Bible Commentary, ed. Tremper Longman III and David E. Garland (Grand Rapids, MI: Zondervan, 2010), 465–74.

34. Jay Adams, *Marriage, Divorce, and Remarriage in the Bible* (Grand Rapids, MI: Zondervan, 1980).

35. Thomas Edgar, "Divorce & Remarriage for Adultery or Desertion," in *Divorce and Remarriage: Four Christian Views*, ed. H. Wayne House (Downers Grove, IL: InterVarsity Press, 1990), 151–96.

36. John Jefferson Davis, *Evangelical Ethics: Issues Facing the Church Today*, 4th ed. (Phillipsburg, NJ: P&R, 2015), 90–105.

37. John S. Feinberg and Paul D. Feinberg, *Ethics for a Brave New World*, 2nd ed. (Wheaton, IL: Crossway, 2010), 583–633.

38. Robertson McQuilkin and Paul Copan, *An Introduction to Biblical Ethics: Walking in the Way of Wisdom*, 3rd ed. (Downers Grove, IL: InterVarsity Press, 2014), 234–48.

mate biblical grounds for divorce? The position that I advocated in my 2018 book, *Christian Ethics*, was that these two were the only legitimate grounds allowed by Scripture.

However, as a result of additional research that I carried out in 2019, I now believe that 1 Corinthians 7:15 implies that divorce may be legitimate in other circumstances that damage the marriage as seriously as adultery or desertion. This change in my position has come because I reached a new understanding of Paul's expression "in such cases."

1. A New and Broader Understanding of "in Such Cases" (1 Cor. 7:15). Here, once again, is the key verse in which Paul allows for divorce in cases of desertion by an unbeliever:

> But if the unbelieving partner separates, let it be so. *In such cases* the brother or sister is not enslaved. God has called you to peace. (1 Cor. 7:15)

The Greek phrase that is translated as "in such cases" is *en tois toioutois*. The phrase does not occur anywhere else in the New Testament, nor does it occur in the Septuagint (the Greek translation of the Old Testament). It does occur in Greek literature outside the Bible, but, so far as I can tell, no interpreter of 1 Corinthians has ever studied its use in extrabiblical literature.[39] Most commentaries just assume that it means "in cases of desertion by

---

39. I could not find any discussion of *en tois toioutois* in literature outside the Bible in any of the numerous academic commentaries on 1 Cor. that I have in my

an unbeliever," which is the specific situation that Paul mentions.

However, I found several examples where this Greek phrase clearly referred to more kinds of situations than the specific situation that the author was discussing. Here are some of those examples:

a. Philo (Jewish author, c. 30 BC–AD 45): In commenting on the 10th plague on Egypt, when the Egyptians discovered that all their firstborn sons and firstborn cattle had been killed, Philo says,

> And, as so often happens *in such cases* [*en tois toioutois*], they thought that their present condition was but the beginning of greater evils, and were filled with fear of the destruction of those who still lived. (*The Life of Moses*, 1.38)

The specific situation that Philo names is the sudden death of their firstborn sons. But "in such cases" cannot be limited to that situation only, because that had never happened before. Yet Philo is referring to something that happens quite often, for he says "as so often happens in such cases." His meaning must be, "as so often happens when sudden tragedy strikes," which is a much broader

---

home library, nor could my teaching assistant Brett Gray find any such research in any of the commentaries in the Phoenix Seminary library.

I do not think any such study would have been possible before the development of the immensely valuable *Thesaurus Linguae Graecae* database at the University of California-Irvine, which did not become available for academic research by outside scholars until the early to mid-1980s.

category than just the death of all the firstborn sons in a nation.

b. Lysias (Greek orator, c. 459–c. 380 BC):

> When Phrynichus had to pay a fine to the Treasury, my father did not bring him his contribution of money: yet it is *in such cases* [*en tois toioutois*], that we see the best proof of a man's friends. (*Pro Polystrato*, 12:4)

In this statement, Lysias cannot be claiming that "the best proof of a man's friends" comes only when someone suddenly has to pay a fine to the Treasury, for such circumstances are uncommon. He must mean that "the best proof of a man's friends" comes when someone suddenly has an unexpected need for money—then you find out who your friends really are. Here again, the expression "in such cases" refers to a much broader category of situations than the specific example named.

c. Euripides (Greek tragedian, c. 480–c. 406 BC):

> But go inside the house at once and make things ready there. Surely a woman, if she wants to, can find many additions to a meal. Really there is still enough in the house to cram them with food for one day at least. It is *in such cases* [*en tois toioutois*] . . . that I see how wealth has great power, to give to strangers, and to expend in curing the body when it falls sick. (*Electra*, line 426)

The specific situation named is a sudden need for food to feed to unexpected guests, but "in such cases" refers more broadly to any situation in which wealth provides the ability to meet unexpected needs.

Other examples could be given,[40] but it should be clear from these examples that, when Paul uses *en tois toioutois* to say that "*in such cases* the brother or sister is not enslaved" (1 Cor. 7:15), he implies that divorce is a legitimate possibility not only in cases of desertion by an unbeliever, but also in other circumstances that are *similar to* but not necessarily exactly like desertion. A reasonable possibility is that "in such cases" in 1 Corinthians 7:15 means "*in this and other similarly destructive situations*" (that is, situations that destroy a marriage as much as adultery or desertion).

A confirming argument comes from Paul's use of the *plural* expression "in such cases," whereas he could have

---

40. See Euripides, *Troiades*, line 303; Diodorus Siculus, *Bibliotheca historica*, 1.23.7; Sophocles, *Electra*, line 990; and Epictetus, *Dissertationes ab Arriano digestae*, 1.1.21.

I did find other examples where "in such cases" referred to a broad category of actions or things that were the same or very similar to the specific situation named (such as Josephus, *Antiquities of the Jews*, 8.379), but none of these examples was exactly parallel to 1 Cor. 7:15 because they all had a *plural* antecedent, which is different from Paul's singular example "if the unbeliever departs." I examined 52 examples of *en tois toioutois* (I chose them because the English translations were most readily available to me), and I did not find one example where the phrase referred to a *singular* antecedent (like 1 Cor. 7:15) and the context implied that "such cases" were limited to situations that were *exactly the same* as the one named by the author.

In addition, several other examples of this phrase were followed by plural nouns that specifically narrowed the range of application, such as "among such people" (*en tois toioutois anthrōpois*, Plato, *Protagoras*, Stephanus, p. 327, d.5) or "in such times" (*en tois toioutois kairois*, Isocrates, *Archidamus* [orat. 6], sec. 34, line 2). These examples were not exactly parallel to 1 Cor. 7:15, where no immediately following noun limited the range of application.

just used the singular expression *en touto* ("in this case") if he had wanted to refer only to the case of desertion by an unbeliever. (He uses the singular phrase in 1 Cor. 11:22 and 2 Cor. 8:10, for example.)

Someone might object that Paul uses a plural expression because he mentions "the brother or sister," which includes two people. But that objection is not persuasive because the sense of the expression "such cases" (*toioutois*) requires that it refer to something previously mentioned (the reader, in processing the phrase, immediately wonders "Such as what?" and looks to the first part of the sentence), and therefore it must refer back to the "if" clause in Paul's argument, "if the unbeliever separates." In addition, Paul treats "brother or sister" as a *single* possibility (the verb *dedoulōtai*, "is not enslaved," is singular), so Paul could have easily used the singular expression *en touto* ("in this case") if he had wanted to refer only to a case of desertion.

2. What Other Kinds of Situations Might Be Harmful Enough to Include in "in Such Cases"?

Paul does not specify a list of any other specific situations in which divorce might be considered legitimate. He must have been aware of Jesus's teaching while on earth, "What therefore God has joined together, let not man separate" (Matt. 19:6), for he says that it is a command from "the Lord" that "the wife should not separate from her husband" and "the husband should not divorce his wife" (1 Cor. 7:10–11). But in this same context, Jesus had also taught that adultery was a legitimate reason—in fact, the only legitimate reason—for divorce (see Matt. 19:9), and Paul no doubt was also aware of that teaching.

a. Paul's Reasoning: In light of this background, what reasoning leads Paul, with his apostolic authority, to add desertion (which was not specified by Jesus) as another legitimate ground for divorce? In order to do this, he must have been persuaded that desertion by an unbeliever destroys a marriage as much as adultery does.[41] Once the unbeliever has departed, the man and woman are no longer living together and no longer acting in any sense as husband and wife. If the deserting spouse is an unbeliever, then he or she is beyond the reach of church discipline, and there is no reasonable human hope that the man and woman will ever again function as if they are husband and wife. The marriage has been destroyed. Recognizing this reality, Paul says, "In such cases the brother or sister is not enslaved" (1 Cor. 7:15). And when he uses the broad category "in such cases," he suggests that other situations might also be included, following the same line of reasoning. We might even consider translating the phrase as "in cases similar to this."

b. "Not Enslaved": Paul gives another indication of the kinds of situations that would fall into this category when he permits divorce by using the unusual expression "is

---

41. David Clyde Jones also sees this as the reason, for, in explaining why adultery and desertion are the two grounds for divorce given in Matt. 19:9 and 1 Cor. 7:15, he writes, "The exceptional circumstance common to both instances is willful and radical violation of the marriage covenant." *Biblical Christian Ethics* (Grand Rapids, MI: Baker, 1994), 202.

not enslaved" (Greek *douloō*, "to enslave"; this is the Greek verb that corresponds to the common noun *doulos*, "slave, bondservant, servant"). The Bible never uses the verb *douloō* anywhere else to refer to marriage, and by using it here Paul implies that forbidding a deserted spouse to be divorced would be akin to trapping that spouse in slavery. But God does not require his children to live for their entire lives in a slavelike situation, Paul assures his readers, because instead of slavery, "God has called you to peace" (Greek *eirēnē*, "peace, harmony, well-being," with echoes of the Old Testament concept of *shālôm*, "peace, well-being").

c. Other Situations That Require Wise Consideration: With this background, we can now ask what other kinds of situations might destroy a marriage to the same extent that adultery or desertion would destroy it, and what other situations would trap a spouse in a slavelike condition that can only be remedied by divorce. Several categories of situations come to mind.

(1) Abuse: If an abused spouse is *forced to flee from the home for self-protection* from ongoing, violent abuse, in my judgment, that would be a situation in which the damage is sufficiently similar to the damage from adultery or desertion that divorce would be a legitimate option.[42] In

---

42. John M. Frame sees abuse as a legitimate ground for divorce in some cases. *The Doctrine of the Christian Life: A Theology of Lordship* (Phillipsburg, NJ: P&R, 2008), 781. David Clyde Jones also thinks that physical abuse so violates the

some ways such abuse is worse than desertion because it in-
volves repeated demonstrations of actual malice, not simply
indifference. Abuse is actively malevolent. And the result
is the same (the couple is no longer together). The abusing
spouse has not technically "deserted," but he or she bears
the moral guilt of *causing* the separation.

This was the view of the church father John Chrysostom
(c. 349–407), in commenting on 1 Corinthians 7:15. He
wrote,

> But what is the meaning of, "if the unbelieving depar-
> teth?" For instance, if he bid thee sacrifice and take part
> in his ungodliness on account of thy marriage, or else
> part company; it were better if the marriage were an-
> nulled, and no breach made in godliness. Wherefore he
> adds, "A brother is not under bondage, nor yet a sister,
> in such cases." If day by day he buffet [*pukteuō*, box,
> punch] thee and keep up combats [*polemos*, war, battle,
> fighting] on this account, it is better to separate. For
> this is what he glances at, saying, "But God has called
> us in peace." For it is the other party who furnished the
> ground of separation, even as he did who committed
> uncleanness [*porneuō*].[43]

Let me be very clear at this point. I am *not* saying that
divorce is legitimate in every case in which a spouse claims

---

marriage covenant that it is a sufficient ground, as well as adultery and desertion,
for divorce. *Biblical Christian Ethics*, 177–204.

43. John Chrysostom, "Homily 19 on 1 Corinthians," in *Nicene and Post
Nicene Fathers*, Series 1, ed. Philip Schaff, 14 vols. (1886–1889; repr., Peabody,
MA: Hendrickson, 1994), 12:108. Hereafter cited as *NPNF*[1].

to be abused (whether physically, or verbally/emotionally, or both). But I am saying that *there are some cases* in which the abuse (whether physical or verbal/emotional) has damaged the marriage as much as adultery or desertion would damage it, and "in such cases" 1 Corinthians 7:15 would apply and divorce would be legitimate. In some cases, even a single instance of abuse may be so violent (even resulting in broken bones and hospitalization) that it would be dangerous for the abused spouse to return, and in such a situation it would be legitimate to seek a divorce.

(2) **Abuse of Children:** The same reasoning would apply if the abuse is directed against the children instead of the spouse.

(3) **Extreme, Prolonged Verbal and Relational Cruelty:** Treatment that is destroying the other spouse's mental and emotional stability could be so severe that it would fall into the category of "in such cases" and would be a legitimate ground for divorce.

(4) **Credible Threats of Serious Physical Harm or Murder:** Dire threats to a spouse or children could also, in some cases, fall into this category.

(5) **Incorrigible Drug or Alcohol Addiction:** Addiction that is accompanied by regular lies, deceptions, thefts, and/or violence might, in some cases, be so destructive to the marriage that it would also fall into this category.

(6) Incorrigible Gambling Addiction: If uncontrolled gambling has led to massive, overwhelming indebtedness, it could also, in some cases, fall into this category.

(7) Incorrigible Addiction to Pornography: This addiction might also fall into this category. However, earlier in this book I included addiction to pornography under the meaning of "sexual immorality" (Greek *porneia*) in Matthew 19:9.

(8) Situations That Are Not Legitimate Grounds for Divorce: In the midst of a secular culture where divorces are far too easy and common, it is good to remember that Scripture does not allow divorce just because a marriage is difficult, because a husband and wife are not getting along, or because one spouse wants to marry another person. We need to be reminded again of the warnings of Jesus that such divorces are contrary to God's will and commonly result in what God considers to be adultery (see Matt. 19:3–9).

d. The Need for Wisdom: Pastors, elders, and Christian counselors, if asked for counsel about whether divorce is a legitimate option in specific cases, need much wisdom and discernment (see Phil. 1:9; James 1:5–6) in order to rightly evaluate the actual degree of harm in individual cases and whether there is a reasonable basis for hope that the destructive behavior has ended and the marriage can be saved. This is why I repeatedly used the words *might* and *could* in the list above. No book on Christian ethics can possibly specify all the complex details that will be part of every real-life situation.

e. Additional Note: Churches Need to Aggressively Protect an Abused Spouse:

I recognize that some readers may not be persuaded by my argument that "in such cases" indicates that Paul thought there were other legitimate grounds for divorce. But all readers should agree that when a situation of abuse becomes known, the church must quickly protect the abused spouse. This should be true in all churches, including those that only recognize two legitimate grounds for divorce.

In a case of physical abuse, *something*—perhaps *several things*—must be done quickly to prevent the abused spouse from having to endure further suffering.[44] As soon as church leaders become aware of a situation of physical abuse, they should act to bring the abuse to an immediate halt, often by encouraging the abused spouse to separate and move to another, perhaps undisclosed, living location (for the eventual purpose of bringing restoration of the marriage along with the complete cessation of the abuse). In addition, other actions may need to be taken, and these

---

44. For specific solutions, see Chris Moles, *The Heart of Domestic Abuse: Gospel Solutions for Men Who Use Control and Violence in the Home* (Bemidji, MN: Focus, 2015). See also Jason Meyer, "A Complementarian Manifesto against Domestic Abuse," The Gospel Coalition, Dec. 2, 2015, https://www.thegospel coalition.org/article/a-complementarian-manifesto-against-domestic-abuse. For compassionate and wise help in bringing healing to victims of abuse, see Steven R. Tracy, *Mending the Soul: Understanding and Healing Abuse* (Grand Rapids, MI: Zondervan, 2005).

will vary from case to case. These actions may include church discipline, confrontation and counseling, police intervention, a court order, and other kinds of intervention by church members, family members, and friends.[45] As I have argued elsewhere,[46] when a person is facing the likelihood of physical assault, self-defense or fleeing from the danger are both morally right actions. In some cases, filing a complaint with local police and pressing charges may also be appropriate, because violently attacking one's spouse and doing physical harm is a criminal act and subject to legal penalties. Using every available means, the abuse must be stopped and the abused spouse must be protected.

Finally, we should recognize that abuse is more than twice as common among couples who live together without getting married compared to married couples who did not live together before marriage. According to a 2015 study by the American College of Pediatricians, citing research done by C. T. Kenney and S. S. McLanahan, the rate of abuse for married couples who remained married was 15.5 percent (a tragically high number). But for cohabitating

---

45. I am aware of at least two situations in which women told my wife, Margaret, and me that in the past they had been physically abused by their husbands and that they had gone to their pastors for help, but the pastors had minimized the problem and sent the women away. This was a tragic and inexcusable shirking of responsibility on the part of those pastors.

But we are also aware of at least one situation in which several people in our church (including my wife and teenage son) helped an abused wife move out of her house in the middle of the day when her husband was at work, after which church discipline was initiated, eventually leading to repentance and reconciliation. More than 10 years after that, the marriage was still healthy.

46. See Grudem, *Christian Ethics*, 551–65 (chap. 20).

couples who did not eventually marry, the percentage was 35.3 percent. Cohabitating couples who eventually got married had a rate of 21.9 percent.[47]

f. Restoration of the Marriage, if Possible, Must Remain the First Goal: After such an extensive discussion of possible grounds for divorce, it is important to remember that God established marriage as a lifelong commitment (see Matt. 19:3–9; 1 Cor. 7:10–14). So long as it is consistent with the necessary protection for an abused spouse, pastors and counselors should first seek to restore a marriage to health and obedience to God's instructions about marriage. If the abusing spouse is a professing Christian, church discipline should be initiated. It will frequently bring a good result and the marriage will be saved.

g. Objections: Several possible objections may be brought against my argument about "in such cases" in 1 Corinthians 7:15.

(1) Objection: "In a case of abuse, why not just counsel lifelong separation without divorce?"

My answer is that this would be leaving the abused spouse "enslaved" to the marriage and to the abusing spouse, but Paul says such a spouse is "not enslaved" in situations like this.

---

47. "Cohabitation: Effects of Cohabitation on the Men and Women Involved— Part 1 of 2," American College of Pediatricians, March 2015, http://www.acpeds .org/the-college-speaks/position-statements/societal-issues/cohabitation-part-1 -of-2, citing C. T. Kenney and S. S. McLanahan, "Why are cohabitating relationships more violent than marriages?" *Demography* 43, no. 1 (February 2006): 127–40.

(2) Objection: "This will open the floodgates to many needless divorces in marriages that could be saved."

My answer is that I am not advocating for "needless divorces." Genuine efforts to save the marriages should be attempted first. But allowing for these additional possible grounds for divorce will save thousands of sincere Christian believers from suffering horrible abuse for decades.

(3) Objection: "Staying in an abusive marriage is a better way to give a witness to society about the goodness of God's plan for lifelong marriage."

Here my answer is that leaving an abusive marriage with the blessing of the church is a better way to give witness to society that God is pleased when we can help to rescue those who suffer unjustly.

(4) Objection: "Sometimes God calls his children to endure suffering. In fact, Peter says, 'If when you do good and suffer for it you endure, this is a gracious thing in the sight of God' (1 Pet. 2:20)."

In response, I agree that God sometimes calls his people to endure suffering, but there is more to the story. God also rescues his people from suffering and calls them to escape from suffering when possible. "I am the LORD your God, who brought you out of the land of Egypt, out of the house of slavery" (Ex. 20:2). "And lead us not into temptation, but deliver us from evil" (Matt. 6:13). "When they persecute you in one town, flee to the next" (Matt. 10:23). "Were you a bondservant when called? Do not be concerned about it. (But if you can gain your freedom, avail yourself of the opportunity)" (1 Cor. 7:21).

h. Conclusion on 1 Corinthians 7:15: Several examples from extrabiblical literature show that the expression "in such cases" (*en tois toioutois*) often refers to a variety of situations that are *similar to* but clearly not identical to the specific situation mentioned. This suggests that Paul considered divorce a legitimate possibility not only in cases of desertion by an unbeliever, but also in situations that similarly brought extensive and severe damage to the marriage.

3. Divorce Because of Material Neglect or Emotional Neglect? David Instone-Brewer argues that, in addition to adultery and desertion by an unbeliever, the New Testament allows divorce for material or emotional neglect. Here is his summary of his position:

> I agree with the two traditional grounds of adultery and desertion by an unbeliever, and two other OT grounds that are alluded to by Paul and Church tradition. These two are emotional neglect and material neglect and are alluded to in 1 Corinthians 7:3–5, 32–34. These two grounds were derived from Exodus 21:10–11, which states that a husband must give a wife food, clothing, and love.[48]

---

48. Instone-Brewer, *Divorce and Remarriage in the Bible*, 275. He has presented the same argument in a more popular book as well, *Divorce and Remarriage in the Church: Biblical Solutions for Pastoral Realities* (Downers Grove, IL: InterVarsity Press, 2003).

Instone-Brewer bases much of his argument on an Old Testament law concerning slaves. In a context of laws concerning a man who has taken a slave woman as his wife, and then takes a second wife, we read:

> If he takes another wife to himself, he shall not diminish her food, her clothing, or her marital rights. And if he does not do these three things for her, she shall go out for nothing, without payment of money. (Ex. 21:10–11)

Instone-Brewer then quotes later rabbinic interpretations that referred to or alluded to this passage when discussing the responsibilities of a husband and wife within marriage. He says that the three categories of "food . . . clothing . . . marital rights"[49] could be summarized as material and emotional support.[50]

He goes on to argue that even the strict rabbinic interpreters, the followers of Shammai, agreed that *failure to provide material or emotional support was a sufficient ground for divorce*.[51] Therefore, the rabbinic quotation that I cited earlier in this book is significant:

> The school of Shammai say: A man may not divorce his wife unless he has found unchastity[52] in her. . . . And

---

49. The phrase "marital rights" was commonly understood to refer to sexual relations within marriage.

50. Instone-Brewer, *Divorce and Remarriage in the Bible*, 100–107.

51. Instone-Brewer, *Divorce and Remarriage in the Bible*, 111–12.

52. The Hebrew wording of the Mishnah here is *debar 'erwat*, "a matter of indecency," which simply borrows two words from Deut. 24:1 (*'erwat dābār*, "some indecency") but reverses the word order.

the school of Hillel say . . . [he may divorce her] even if she spoiled a dish for him. . . . Rabbi Akiba says, [he may divorce her] even if he found another fairer than she. (Mishnah, *Gittin* 9:10)

Instone-Brewer argues as follows:

1. All Jewish interpreters at the time of Christ accepted neglect of the three categories of Exodus 21:10–11 (food, clothing, marital rights) as legitimate grounds for divorce (pp. 100–109).
2. Therefore, the followers of Shammai (the "Shammites") accepted the three grounds of Exodus 21:10–11, and these were included in their understanding of "unchastity" (or "some indecency") in Deuteronomy 24:1 (p. 111).
3. Jesus was quoting Deuteronomy 24:1 when he prohibited divorce "except for sexual immorality" (*mē epi porneia*, Matt. 19:9) and "except on the ground of sexual immorality" (*parektos logou porneias*, Matt. 5:32) (pp. 158–59, 185–87).
4. Jesus nowhere denied the three grounds for divorce in Exodus 21:10–11, and "If Jesus said nothing about a universally accepted belief, then it is assumed by most scholars that this indicated his agreement with it" (p. 185).
5. Therefore, Jesus must have agreed with the strict Shammite view, that divorce was allowed both for adultery and also for neglect of the three obligations in Exodus 21:10–11 (pp. 159, 167, 184).

6. In summary, Jesus allowed divorce not only because of adultery but also because of failure to provide food, clothing, and marital rights (which may be summarized as material or emotional neglect).

In response, while I wish to affirm my appreciation for Instone-Brewer as a gracious friend who has helped me on numerous occasions with research at Tyndale House in Cambridge, England, and also as a meticulous scholar with vast knowledge of the ancient world, I still must confess that I do not find his argument on this matter to be persuasive, for several reasons:

1. While he provides evidence that many Jewish interpreters referred to Exodus 21:10–11 to teach about *the responsibilities of a husband and wife in marriage*, I could not find evidence on pages 100–109 of Instone-Brewer's book that *all* Jewish interpreters agreed that the neglect of food, clothing, or marital rights was *a ground for divorce*.

2. I could find no evidence in his discussion on pages 100–109 that specifically demonstrated that the followers of Shammai held that neglect of food, clothing, or marital rights was *a ground* for divorce, or that the Shammites believed that "some indecency" in Deuteronomy 24:1 included neglect of food, clothing, or marital rights.

3. The argument that Jesus is quoting Deuteronomy 24:1 when he speaks of "sexual immorality" in Matthew 5:32 and 19:9 is not persuasive. The Septuagint does not use *porneia* to translate *'erwat dābār* ("some indecency"), but *aschēmon pragma* ("an indecent or shameful thing"), and this suggests

that the Greek-speaking Jews at the time of Christ would not have heard the term *porneia* as a reference to Deuteronomy 24:1. In addition, the word *porneia* was used to refer to various kinds of sexual intercourse outside of the legitimate bounds of marriage (including adultery), but adultery at the time when Deuteronomy 24:1 was written would have required the death penalty, not divorce (Lev. 20:10; Deut. 22:22). Therefore, it is highly unlikely that Jesus's hearers would have thought he was referring to Deuteronomy 24:1 when he said "except for sexual immorality."[53]

4. It is not enough to say that Jesus did not deny the three grounds for divorce found in Exodus 21:10–11, and therefore he must have agreed with them. Instone-Brewer admits that this is an argument "from silence" (p. 184), but I think it is even weaker than an argument from silence. It is an argument *contrary to* what Jesus explicitly says.

In the context of answering a question from the Pharisees, "Is it lawful to divorce one's wife *for any cause?*" (Matt. 19:3), after Jesus says, "Because of your hardness of heart Moses *allowed* you to divorce your wives, but from the beginning it was not so" (v. 8), we expect Jesus to teach a more strict view of divorce than the very lenient interpretations of Deuteronomy 24 that were promoted by the rabbis. He gives no hint indicating that he is endorsing various views of divorce promoted by different Jewish teachers.

---

53. Earlier in this book, I argued that Jesus, in Matt. 19:9, was *rejecting* the highly permissive grounds for divorce found in some rabbinic interpretations of Deut. 24:1. But his *allowance* for divorce for "sexual immorality" (*porneia*) was not based on Deut. 24:1 because sexual immorality at the time of Moses would have resulted in the death penalty, not in a divorce.

In that context, Jesus explicitly excludes all other grounds for divorce, for he explicitly says:

> Whoever divorces his wife, except for sexual immorality, and marries another, commits adultery. (Matt. 19:9)

The construction "Whoever . . . except for" explicitly rules out all of the grounds for divorce other than adultery. It is not just that Jesus failed to explicitly deny that divorce was valid for failure to provide food, clothing, or marital rights. He also failed to explicitly deny that divorce was valid for a wife spoiling a meal or because a man found another woman whom he thought more beautiful than his present wife. He did not need to deny any of these explicitly because he was denying them all at once when he said, "*Whoever* divorces his wife, except for sexual immorality . . ."

5. Therefore, I do not find that Instone-Brewer has provided convincing evidence that Jesus allowed divorce for neglect of the three obligations in Exodus 21:10–11 (failure to provide food, clothing, or marital rights). Jesus did not teach that divorce was allowed for material or emotional neglect.[54] In the light of contrary evidence about what Jesus clearly *did* teach, an argument based on what Jesus did *not* say has dubious validity.

---

54. I should add that Instone-Brewer's book is an immensely valuable resource for information about divorce and remarriage in ancient Jewish, Greek, and Roman writings, and also for an extensive categorization of a variety of ancient and modern positions on divorce, with detailed documentation for authors who hold each position (pp. 268–99). In addition, from beginning to end, the book gives evidence of genuine and wise pastoral care for people who are experiencing or have experienced divorce.

6. Finally, it is important to step back and remember how far removed Instone-Brewer's argument is from the direct teaching of the New Testament. His argument is based on Exodus 21:10–11, but that is part of the Mosaic covenant, which is no longer in force for the new covenant age.[55] In addition, that passage is not about marriage and divorce in general, but about the rights of a slave woman who has been taken as a man's wife. And the argument is based not on the direct teaching of the passage but on later Jewish application of the passage to the question of divorce, and not just on any Jewish application of the passage, but on the supposed application by the strict followers of Shammai, for which there is no specific documented evidence. And then it is based not on Jesus's explicit affirmation of this supposed view of the Shammites regarding Exodus 21:10–11, but on the fact that Jesus did not explicitly deny this view in his teaching.

Therefore, this position seems to me to be based on something that Jesus did not say about a view of the Shammites that is not documented about a passage that is talking about slavery laws and not about marriage and divorce in general, a passage that is found in the laws of the Mosaic covenant, which is no longer in force. Therefore, this position does not have nearly enough evidence to be persuasive.

4. Divorce Because the Marriage Can't Be Repaired?

Should a divorce be granted when a husband and wife have

---

55. See Grudem, *Christian Ethics*, 209–63 (chap. 8).

been strongly alienated from each other for many months or years, and their entrenched hostility against each other has not responded to repeated attempts at counseling and reconciliation? In such a situation, people who know the couple might say that the marriage is beyond repair.

Craig Blomberg apparently advocated this position for severely damaged marriages. He wrote:

> Perhaps the best way of describing when divorce and remarriage are permitted, then, is to say simply that it is when an individual, in agreement with a supportive Christian community of which that individual has been an intimate part, believes that he or she has no other choice or option in trying to avoid some greater evil. All known attempts at reconciliation have been exhausted.[56]

Blomberg's article demonstrates admirable compassion for people in painful marital situations and for those who already have been divorced. I sympathize with his desire to bring a solution to a deeply dysfunctional situation. I was not persuaded by Blomberg's argument as published, because his argument did not seem to be adequately grounded

---

56. Craig Blomberg, "Marriage, Divorce, Remarriage, and Celibacy: An Exegesis of Matthew 19:3–12," *TrinJ*, n.s., 11 (1990): 193.

Larry Richards also believes that Scripture allows for divorce when a husband and wife decide that "the marriage is really over and it is time to divorce." He argues, "No ecclesiastical court has ever been granted the biblical right to determine who can and cannot divorce," and he would allow for divorce because of hard-heartedness as displayed by "mental and physical abuse, sexual abuse, repeated adulteries, and emotional and spiritual abandonment of the relationship." "Divorce & Remarriage under a Variety of Circumstances," in *Divorce and Remarriage: Four Christian Views*, 242.

in Scripture. However, I expect that some of the situations that Blomberg has in mind would fit into the category of "in such cases" that I now see in 1 Corinthians 7:15.

5. Divorce Because of Incompatibility? Many divorces today are granted not because of adultery, desertion, physical abuse, or material or emotional neglect, but because of some kind of "incompatibility"—the husband and wife are not getting along and no longer want to be married to each other. According to a report by the National Fatherhood Initiative, one survey indicated that the most common reasons for divorce were as follows:

1. Lack of commitment: cited by 73 percent, who said they wished their ex-spouses had "worked harder" to stay married.
2. Arguing: cited by 56 percent.
3. Infidelity: cited by 55 percent.
4. Marrying too young: cited by 46 percent. According to the report, the Centers for Disease Control and Prevention states that nearly 50 percent of teenage marriages fail in the first 15 years.
5. Unrealistic expectations: cited by 45 percent.
6. Lack of "equality": cited by 44 percent.
7. Lack of preparation: cited by 41 percent.
8. Abuse: cited by 29 percent.[57]

---

57. "With This Ring, A National Survey on Marriage," National Fatherhood Initiative, 2005, 32, http://wyofams.org/index_htm_files/NationalMarriageSurvey.pdf. Many of the divorced couples surveyed noted several reasons that led to their divorce, so the percentages here add up to more than 100 percent.

In Europe, the most common reasons cited for divorce by couples are fairly similar, but also include some additional factors, such as substance abuse (50 percent), health problems (27.8 percent), and religious differences (33.3 percent).[58]

It should be clear from the previous discussion, however, that God considers marriage to be a solemn, lifelong commitment, and only the most serious kinds of destructive misconduct (adultery or desertion) are counted as valid grounds for divorce in the teaching of the New Testament.

F. QUESTIONS ABOUT SPECIFIC SITUATIONS

1. People Who Have Been Divorced for Unbiblical Reasons. What should be done if someone has been divorced for reasons other than those given in the Bible and then has married someone else? Jesus says that in such a case the person has committed "adultery," so the marriage began with adultery:

> And I say to you: whoever divorces his wife, except for sexual immorality, and marries another, commits adultery. (Matt. 19:9)

But after such a couple has been married, if they decide they want to follow the teachings of Scripture, what should they do?

---

58. Shelby B. Scott et al., "Reasons for Divorce and Recollections of Premarital Intervention: Implications for Improving Relationship Education," *Couple and Family Psychology* 2, no. 2 (June 2013): 131–45, https://www.ncbi.nlm.nih.gov /pmc/articles/PMC4012696/.

When Jesus says "and marries another" in that same verse, he implies that the second marriage is in fact a true marriage. Jesus does not say, "and *lives outside of marriage* with another" (which was possible),[59] but "and *marries another.*" Therefore, once a second marriage has occurred, it would be further sin to break it up, for it would be destroying another marriage.

This means that the second marriage should not be thought of as a man and a woman living in continual adultery, *for they are now married to each other*, not to anyone else. Yes, Jesus teaches that the marriage began with adultery, but his words also indicate that these two people are now married.[60] The responsibility of the husband and wife in such a case is to ask God for his forgiveness for their previous sin, and also for his blessing on their current

---

59. See the story of the woman at the well in John 4, to whom Jesus says, "You have had five husbands, and the one you now have is not your husband" (v. 18).

60. Here are two analogies that may help people to understand how marriage could *begin* with adultery but, once it has begun, should not be seen as two people living in adultery:

First, some people think that the American War of Independence (1776–1783) was not a just war, but was a morally wrongful rebellion against Great Britain (I do not agree with this viewpoint). But such people would not argue that Americans today are still living in a state of sinful rebellion against the British government. Once the government of the United States was established, it became a separate country, and it is now morally right for it to continue as a separate country.

Second, suppose some parents have an unusually bright daughter and, when they move to a new city, they lie about her birthdate so she can start first grade. She does very well in school, both academically and socially, but then, before the next school year begins, they feel convicted about their wrongdoing and confess it to the principal. Should the school make her attend first grade all over again? No, that would be useless. Her first-grade education began with a lie, but it was still a genuine first-grade education and should be considered legitimate. Her schooling began with a sinful act, but there is no sin involved in counting her as a legitimate student for all her subsequent years of schooling.

marriage. Then they should strive to make the current marriage a good and lasting one.

2. Can Divorced People Ever Become Church Officers?

When Paul lists the qualifications for elders, he includes this statement:

> Therefore an overseer must be above reproach, *the husband of one wife*, sober-minded, self-controlled, respectable, hospitable, able to teach . . . (1 Tim. 3:2)

Similarly, he writes this to Titus about choosing elders:

> This is why I left you in Crete, so that you might put what remained into order, and appoint elders in every town as I directed you—if anyone is above reproach, *the husband of one wife*, and his children are believers and not open to the charge of debauchery or insubordination. (Titus 1:5–6)

This is also a requirement for deacons:

> Let deacons each be *the husband of one wife*, managing their children and their own households well. (1 Tim. 3:12)

a. The Qualifications All Refer to a Man's Present Life and Character:

Sometimes people think that these requirements refer to a man who has not been married more than once, and therefore that they exclude from the offices of elder and deacon all men who have been divorced for whatever reason and then remarried, and also all whose wives have died and who have remarried.

A better understanding of this passage is that it refers to the *present status* of a man, either to his *character* of being faithful to his wife or else to the fact that he is not a polygamist—he does not have more than one wife *at the present time*. In either of these interpretations, the verse does not prohibit all divorced men from being elders or deacons.

In favor of the view that these passages mean a man should be "the husband of one wife" *at the present time* is the fact that *all of the other qualifications* for being an elder or deacon in these contexts refer to a man's *present character*, not his entire past life. This becomes evident when we examine the full list of qualifications for elders in 1 Timothy 3 (I have put in italics the other qualifications that do not necessarily refer to a man's entire previous lifetime, especially those who do not become Christians until sometime during their adult lives):

> The saying is trustworthy: If anyone aspires to the office of overseer, he desires a noble task. Therefore an overseer must be *above reproach*, the husband of one wife, *sober-minded, self-controlled, respectable, hospitable, able to teach, not a drunkard, not violent but gentle, not quarrelsome, not a lover of money*. He must *manage his own household well*, with all dignity *keeping his children submissive*, for if someone does not know how to manage his own household, how will he

care for God's church? He must *not be a recent convert*, or he may become puffed up with conceit and fall into the condemnation of the devil. Moreover, he must be *well thought of by outsiders*, so that he may not fall into disgrace, into a snare of the devil. (1 Tim. 3:1–7)

All the other qualifications that Paul lists refer to a man's *present status*, not his entire past life. For example, Paul does not mean "one who has *never been* violent," but "one who is *not now* violent, but gentle." He does not mean "one who has *never been* a lover of money," but "one who is *not now* a lover of money." He does not mean "one who has been above reproach *for his whole life*," but "one who is *now* above reproach." If we made these qualifications apply to a person's entire past life, then we would exclude from office almost everyone who becomes a Christian as an adult, for it is doubtful that any non-Christian could meet these qualifications.

b. It Is No Character Flaw if a Man's Wife Dies and Then He Marries Again: Another argument in support of this position is that Paul clearly encourages *widows* to marry again: "So I would have younger widows marry" (1 Tim. 5:14). Therefore, there would seem to be no moral short-coming or character flaw simply because a man marries again after his wife dies (see also 1 Cor. 7:39, encouraging remarriage). Therefore, there is no legitimate reason for excluding such a man from becoming an elder or deacon if he is otherwise qualified.

c. These Passages Probably Prohibit a Polygamist from Being an Elder or Deacon:

A better interpretation is that Paul is prohibiting a polygamist (a man who *presently* has more than one wife) from being an elder or deacon. Several reasons support this view: (1) Paul could have said "having been married only once," but he did not.[61] (2) We would have to prevent remarried widowers from being elders or deacons if we take the phrase to mean "having been married only once." But the qualifications for church officers are all based on a man's moral and spiritual character, and there is nothing in Scripture to suggest that a man who remarries after his wife dies has lower moral or spiritual qualifications.[62] (3) Polygamy was possible in the first century. Although it was not common, it was practiced, especially among the Jews. The Jewish historian Josephus says,

---

61. The Greek expression translated as "having been married only once" is *hapax gegamēmenos*, using the word "once" (*hapax*) and a perfect participle of *gameō*, "to marry," giving the sense "having been married once and continuing in the state resulting from that marriage." (Such a construction with *hapax* plus a perfect participle is found, for example, in Heb. 10:2, and a similar construction is found in Heb. 9:26. Related expressions with aorist verbs are found in Heb. 6:4; 9:28; and Jude 3.)

Paul also could have expressed the idea of having been married only once by using a perfect participle of *ginomai* to say "having been a husband of one wife" (*gegonōs mias gunaikos anēr*).

62. Some interpreters in the early church did try to exclude remarried widowers from church office (see, for example, *Apostolic Constitutions* 2.2; 6.17 [third or fourth century AD], and *Apostolic Canons* 17 [fourth or fifth century AD]), but these statements reflect not a biblical perspective but a false asceticism that held that celibacy in general was superior to marriage. (These texts can be found in Alexander Roberts and James Donaldson, eds., *The Ante-Nicene Fathers*, 10 vols. (1885–1887; repr., Peabody, MA: Hendrickson, 1994), 7:396, 457, and 501. Hereafter cited as *ANF*.)

However, Chrysostom (d. AD 407) understood 1 Tim. 3:2 to prohibit polygamy, not second marriages after death or divorce (see his *Homily X* on 1 Tim. 3:1–4 in *NPNF¹*, 13:438).

"For it is an ancestral custom of ours to have several wives at the same time."[63] Rabbinic legislation also regulated inheritance customs and other aspects of polygamy.[64]

Therefore, it is reasonable to understand "the husband of one wife" to prohibit a polygamist from holding the office of elder or deacon.[65] The passages then say nothing about divorce and remarriage with respect to qualifications for church office.

If this is the correct understanding of the phrase, then it has significant practical application in missionary contexts even today in cultures where polygamy is still practiced. The Bible would not encourage a husband to divorce any of his multiple wives, which would leave them without support and protection. But it would not allow a man with multiple wives to be an elder or deacon. This restriction would provide a pattern that, if followed, would generally lead to the abolition of polygamy in a church in a generation or two.

d. Another Possibility Is That These Passages Mean a Man Must Be "Faithful to His Wife": An alternative view of

---

63. Josephus, *Antiquities of the Jews*, 17.14; in 17.19 he lists the nine women who were married to King Herod at the same time. An English translation can be found in Josephus, *Antiquities of the Jews*, trans. Ralph Marcus (Cambridge, MA: Harvard University Press, and London: Heinemann, 1969), 8:379 and 381.

64. See Mishnah, *Yebamoth* 4:11; *Ketuboth* 10:1, 4, 5; *Sanhedrin* 2:4; *Kerithoth* 3:7; *Kiddushin* 2:7; *Bechoroth* 8:4 (the Mishnah reflects much oral tradition going back to the first century or earlier). Other evidence on Jewish polygamy is found in Justin Martyr, *Dialogue with Trypho*, chap. 134, *ANF*, 1:266–67. Evidence for polygamy among non-Jews is not as extensive but is indicated in Herodotus (d. 420 BC), *History*, 1.135; 4.155; 2 Macc. 4:30 (about 170 BC); Tertullian, *Apology* 46, in *ANF*, 3:50–51.

65. This is also the view of Davis, *Evangelical Ethics*, 103.

these passages claims that the expression *mias gunaikos andra*, "husband of one wife," means "having the character of a one-woman man"; that is, "faithful to his wife." In support of this view is the fact that a similar phrase is used in 1 Timothy 5:9 for qualifications for widows (Greek, *henos andros gunē*: "one-man woman," i.e., "wife of one husband"):

> Let a widow be enrolled if she is not less than sixty years of age, *having been the wife of one husband*.

In this verse, "wife of one husband" seems to refer to the trait of faithfulness, for a prohibition of remarriage after the death of a spouse would be in contradiction to Paul's advice in 1 Timothy 5:14, "I would have younger widows marry." In addition, it would not make sense for "wife of one husband" to mean a woman could not be married to more than one man at the same time (polyandry), for that was unknown in Jewish or Greco-Roman cultures. Therefore, it is argued that verse 9 must mean "having been faithful to her husband." The commentators who favor the view that 3:2 means "faithful to his wife" all seem to be swayed by this parallel expression in 5:9.[66]

---

66. The majority of modern commentators seem to favor the explanation that says "husband of one wife" means "having the character of a one-woman man," that is, a man who is faithful to his wife. See George Knight III, *Commentary on the Pastoral Epistles*, New International Greek Testament Commentaries (Grand Rapids, MI: Eerdmans, 1992), 157–59; also I. Howard Marshall, *The Pastoral Epistles*, International Critical Commentary (Edinburgh: T&T Clark, 1999), 250–51. The most extensive discussion of different options for "husband of one wife" is found in William Mounce, *Pastoral Epistles*, Word Biblical Commentary 46 (Nashville: Thomas Nelson, 2000), 170–73.

But I do not find this supposed parallel to be very persuasive, because the context is different, the reason for the requirement is different, and the tense of the Greek verbs used in the longer sentence is different in each case. (Commentators do not generally take account of these differences.) In addition, there is a common Greek word meaning "faithful" (the adjective *pistos*), a word that Paul uses several times in 1 Timothy, and he easily could have used this word in 1 Timothy 3:2 if he had wanted to say "faithful to his wife." But he did not.

It is natural that "having been the wife of one husband" (1 Tim. 5:9) would refer to the entire *past life* of a widow, because Paul is talking about requirements for receiving financial support from the church: a woman who had been married to more than one husband would have had more extended family members who could provide support for her. And all of the requirements for widows to receive financial support in 1 Timothy 5:9–10 have to do with their entire *past lives*, not their present lives and characters, as is the case in the requirements for elders and deacons in chapter 3.[67] This is why many English translations render the requirement for a widow in 1 Timothy 5:9 as "*having been the wife of one husband*" (ESV, NASB, RSV, KJV) all refer-

---

67. This contextual focus on a widow's past life makes the translation "having been the wife of one husband" appropriate, and this is even more true if we understand the force of the perfect participle *gegonuia* in 1 Tim. 5:9 to carry over from the previous phrase. In any case, all the qualifications for enrolling widows in 1 Tim. 5:9–10 speak of past history in their lives. But in 1 Tim. 3:2 and Titus 1:6, the sense is different, because present-tense forms of *eimi* ("to be") are used: "an overseer must *be* above reproach, the husband of one wife" (1 Tim. 3:2).

ring to past life (similarly, NIV says "has been"; NLT says "was faithful"), but translate the requirement for elders in 1 Timothy 3:2 as "an overseer must *be* . . . the husband of one wife" (referring to present life).

But I appreciate the weight of the arguments for the "faithful to his wife" interpretation also. And whether someone holds to the "not a polygamist" interpretation or the "faithful to his wife" interpretation, it is clear that Paul is not speaking about all second marriages. He is not prohibiting from church leadership a man whose wife has died and who has remarried, or a man who has been divorced and who has remarried (these cases should be evaluated on an individual basis).

e. Do the Qualifications for Leadership Require That Elders and Deacons Must Be Married? When Paul says that an elder or deacon must be the "husband of one wife," it is unlikely that he means that every elder or deacon must be married, for two reasons:

1. Both Jesus and Paul (1 Cor. 7:7–8; 9:5) were single, and it is unlikely that Paul would have given a requirement for eldership that not even he or Jesus himself could fulfill.

2. Paul also gives requirements about children, saying that an elder must be someone whose "*children* are believers" (Titus 1:6) and "he must manage his own household well, with all dignity keeping his *children* submissive" (1 Tim. 3:4). He says that deacons must be "managing their *children* and their own households well" (1 Tim. 3:12). It is unlikely that Paul is requiring that elders must have two

or more children (the nouns are plural, implying more than one). Rather, it seems that Paul is speaking about the most common kind of situation, a married man with children, and the sense of the passage is, "*If he has children*, the children should be believers and submissive to their parents."

Similarly, the "husband of one wife" passages should be understood to mean, "*If he is married*, he should have only one wife" (or "he should be faithful to his wife"). That would be the most common situation for an elder or deacon, and Paul is speaking about the ordinary cases, giving a picture of the typical approved overseer or deacon as a faithful husband and father, and not absolutely requiring marriage or children.

3. Should Laws about Divorce Reflect Biblical Standards? It is appropriate to comment briefly on a question about civil laws. Should Christians seek to influence laws so that they reflect biblical standards regarding marriage and divorce?

Since marriage is not an institution only for Christians, but is an institution established by God at creation (Gen. 1:27–28; 2:24–25), God intended it to apply to all people, believers and unbelievers alike, and he intended it to be beneficial both to individual husbands and wives, and to society in general.[68]

Therefore, the standards expressed in Scripture regarding divorce and remarriage are the standards that are ultimately best for all people, according to the purpose of our

---

68. See further discussion in Grudem, *Christian Ethics*, 710–12.

Creator. It seems to me, therefore, that the church, where it has opportunity, should give personal encouragement to non-Christians as well as Christians to abide by God's high moral standards regarding divorce and remarriage, and should encourage legislative proposals that would provide more legal support for the solemnity of marriage and its intended lifelong commitment; assistance for troubled marriages; more protection for spouses who sincerely seek to repair their marriages; and provisions for temporary separation and permanent divorce when it is clear that no other solution is possible.

In addition, in societies and cultures where rampant divorce for all sorts of reasons has been occurring for decades, individual Christians as well as churches should also seek to support and minister to women, men, and children who have been hurt by divorces in the past.

G. EVALUATION OF MORE RESTRICTIVE VIEWS REGARDING DIVORCE AND REMARRIAGE

While the position on divorce and remarriage that I have supported in this book has been the most common one among conservative Protestants since the Reformation, and while I have discussed the views of other authors who have *less restrictive* positions (they allow additional grounds for divorce), we also must analyze at this point the positions of some other authors who hold *more restrictive* views of divorce and remarriage. There are two categories of more

restrictive views: (1) no divorce and no remarriage, and
(2) divorce but no remarriage.

1. No Divorce and No Remarriage. J. Carl Laney argues
that the Bible never approves of divorce and, if a divorce
occurs, remarriage to someone else is never permitted. He
says, "I believe Scripture teaches that marriage was designed
by God to be permanent unto death, and that divorce and
remarriage constitute the sin of adultery."[69]

Laney emphasizes Jesus's teaching on the permanence
of marriage in Matthew 19:4–6 (p. 32), and especially
Jesus's statement, "What therefore God has joined together, let not man separate" (v. 6). In answer to the
question of the Pharisees, "Is it lawful to divorce one's
wife for any cause?" (v. 3), Laney says that Jesus's answer "indicates, 'There is no valid reason at all' for divorce" (p. 33).[70]

---

69. J. Carl Laney, "No Divorce and No Remarriage," in *Divorce and Remarriage: Four Christian Views*, 16. This chapter is a summary of Laney's earlier book,
The Divorce Myth: A Biblical Examination of Divorce and Remarriage (Minneapolis, MN: Bethany House, 1981). More recently, the "no divorce-no remarriage"
position has been defended by my friend Gordon J. Wenham in his book *Jesus,
Divorce, and Remarriage* (Bellingham, WA: Lexham, 2019).

70. I might add at this point that "no divorce" is also the historic position
of the Roman Catholic Church. See *Catechism of the Catholic Church*, 2nd ed.
(New York: Doubleday, 1997), para. 1650, 2382–86. "A rectified and consum-
mated marriage cannot be dissolved by any human power or for any reason other
than death" (para. 2382). "Divorce is a grave offense against the natural law. . . .
Contracting a new union, even if it is recognized by civil law, adds to the gravity
of the rupture: the remarried spouse is then in a situation of public and permanent
adultery" (para. 2384). As for those who have been divorced and then married
someone else, "they cannot receive Eucharistic communion as long as this situation
persists" (para. 1650).

However, the catechism also includes another statement that seems to allow for
divorce in several specific circumstances: "If civil divorce remains the only possible
way of ensuring certain legal rights, the care of the children, or the protection of

What then shall we make of the phrase "except for sexual immorality" in Matthew 19:9?

> And I say to you: whoever divorces his wife, *except for sexual immorality* [Greek, *porneia*], and marries another, commits adultery.

Laney says that *porneia* in this verse refers to incest, and this means that Jesus was allowing divorce in the case of a marriage to a close relative, as defined in Leviticus 18:6–18. Laney writes, "The exception clause in Matthew 19:9 simply states that Christ's prohibition against divorce (Mt 19:6) does not apply in the case of an illegal, incestuous marriage" (p. 35). He points out that *porneia* refers to incest in 1 Corinthians 5:1.

I do not find Laney's argument persuasive. The term *porneia* is quite common (75 instances in the New Testament and Septuagint combined, 25 in the New Testament alone) and can be used to refer to any kind of "unlawful sexual intercourse."[71] Laney himself agrees that the term "basically refers to unlawful sexual activity, including prostitution, unchastity and fornication. *Porneia* is a general term which can be interpreted in various ways" (p. 34).

Therefore, it is highly unlikely that Matthew or the Greek-speaking readers of Matthew's Gospel would have

---

inheritance, it can be tolerated and does not constitute a moral offense" (para. 2383). I do not understand how this statement is consistent with the other statements I quoted that strictly prohibit divorce.

71. Bauer et al., *A Greek-English Lexicon of the New Testament*, 854.

understood "sexual immorality" (*porneia*) to be restricted to the kinds of incest described in Leviticus 18:6–18, especially when the term *porneia* does not even occur in the Septuagint translation of that passage. There is no clearly restrictive wording in these passages, such as "except for sexual immorality *with members of one's own family*," that would signal readers that Jesus is using the word in a highly restrictive sense here. The fact that *porneia* is used in one verse to refer to incest (1 Cor. 5:1) does not nullify the evidence from many other passages in both the Old Testament and New Testament showing that the word refers to a wide range of immoral sexual activity, so that is the sense we should give it in Matthew 19:9 as well.

Instone-Brewer points out:

> [Understanding *porneia* to mean "incest" in Matthew 19:9] would not make good sense in the context of Jesus's teaching. Jesus was criticizing those who use a divorce certificate too freely. . . . In the case of incest, however, there is no need for a divorce certificate because the marriage would be considered invalid from the start. The rabbis did not consider that any marriage had taken place.[72]

My conclusion is that the "no divorce and no remarriage" view cannot adequately account for the precise

---

72. *Divorce and Remarriage in the Bible*, 158. Instone-Brewer also argues that more recent analysis of the linguistic evidence from Qumran, to which Joseph Fitzmyer appealed and to which Laney also appeals, shows that *porneia* should not be understood to apply strictly to incest (pp. 157–58).

wording found in Matthew 19:9 and 1 Corinthians 7:15, where divorce is allowed for adultery and for desertion.

2. Divorce but No Remarriage. In 1990, William Heth argued that even though divorces sometimes will occur, remarriage to another person is never justified. Heth later changed his position,[73] as I explain later (pp. 84–85), but his 1990 argument still remains a widely accessible, articulate defense of this position, and it is still profitable to understand it and interact with it.

A crucial point in Heth's earlier argument was his explanation of Matthew 19:9: "And I say to you: whoever divorces his wife, except for sexual immorality, and marries another, commits adultery."

Heth claimed that the phrase "except for sexual immorality" only applied to the first part of the sentence ("whoever divorces his wife"), but not to the second part of the sentence ("and marries another"). He wrote:

> Matthew 19:9 contains two conditional statements, one that is qualified and one that is unqualified or absolute: (1) A man may not divorce his wife unless she

---

73. See William Heth, "Jesus on Divorce: How My Mind Has Changed," *Southern Baptist Journal of Theology* 6, no. 1 (Spring 2002): 4–29. But Heth's coauthor, Gordon Wenham, continued to hold the divorce but no remarriage view; see Wenham, "Does the New Testament Approve Remarriage after Divorce?" *Southern Baptist Journal of Theology* 6, no. 1 (Spring 2002), 30–45. Wenham emphasizes that this was apparently the unanimous view of the church in the second century AD, and doubts that they all could have misread the New Testament texts and forgotten apostolic teaching so quickly (p. 41). See also Wenham and Heth, *Jesus and Divorce: Towards an Evangelical Understanding of New Testament Teaching*, 2nd ed. (Carlisle, UK: Paternoster, 2002).

is guilty of adultery, and (2) Whoever marries another woman after divorcing his wife commits adultery. Or to paraphrase the idea another way: "Divorcing for reasons other than marital unfaithfulness is forbidden, and remarriage after every divorce is adulterous."[74]

However, I do not find Heth's explanation to be a plausible understanding of Matthew 19:9. This is because he fails to account for the fact that there is one subject ("whoever," or *hos an* in Greek) for all three verbs:

---

74. William Heth, "Divorce, but No Remarriage," in *Divorce and Remarriage: Four Christian Views*, 104. This chapter is a summary of Heth's longer argument in William Heth and Gordon J. Wenham, *Jesus and Divorce: The Problem with the Evangelical Consensus* (Nashville: Thomas Nelson, 1984).

Another thoughtful and carefully reasoned defense of the "no remarriage" position is found in a paper by John Piper, "Divorce & Remarriage: A Position Paper," Desiring God, July 21, 1986, http://www.desiringgod.org/articles/divorce-remarriage-a-position-paper. Piper's arguments are, as one might expect, exceptionally clear and forceful. He places much weight on what he sees as the clear prohibition of remarriage in several other New Testament passages and on the possible alternative explanations for Matt. 19:9. Although I count John as a valued lifelong friend, and although I agree with nearly everything he teaches, I respectfully disagree with him on this topic.

Piper also notes that the official position of the church he pastored at the time, adopted by its Council of Deacons in 1989, differs with his own "no remarriage" position. The church's position includes these statements: "Divorce may be permitted when a spouse deserts the relationship, commits adultery, or is dangerously abusive (1 Cor. 7:15; Matthew 19:9; 1 Cor. 7:11). . . . The remarriage of the aggrieving, divorced spouse may be viewed as severing the former marriage so that the unmarried spouse whose behavior did not biblically justify being divorced, may be free to remarry a believer (Matthew 19:9). . . . After serious efforts have been made toward reconciliation the aggrieved partners referred to in guideline #3 may, together with the leadership of the church, come to regard their marriages as irreparably broken. In such cases remarriage may be a legitimate step, if taken with serious reckoning that this cuts off all possibility of a reconciliation that God may yet be willing to produce." See "A Statement on Divorce & Remarriage in the Life of Bethlehem Baptist Church," Desiring God, May 2, 1989, http://www.desiringgod.org/articles/a-statement-on-divorce-remarriage-in-the-life-of-bethlehem-baptist-church. Piper also discusses the divorce passages in *What Jesus Demands from the World* (Wheaton, IL: Crossway, 2006), 301–22.

whoever divorces . . . and marries . . . commits adultery.

But Heth's explanation wrongly introduces two different subjects, and this illegitimately turns the verse into two separate statements, as his explanation shows:

1. *A man* may not divorce his wife unless she is guilty of adultery, and
2. *Whoever* marries another woman after divorcing his wife commits adultery.[75]

This is not what Jesus said. He did not make two separate statements on two different subjects, but made one statement about "whoever":

And I say to you: *whoever divorces* his wife, except for sexual immorality, *and marries* another, *commits adultery*. (Matt. 19:9)

In order to do justice to this verse, it is best to conclude, as I did earlier, that Jesus is saying that a man who divorces his wife because of sexual immorality and marries another woman does not commit adultery. In other words, Jesus permits remarriage in this case.

Another difficulty with Heth's earlier understanding is that, on his explanation, Matthew 19:9 does not make sense. As we noted earlier, if we remove the clause "and

---

75. Heth, "Divorce, but No Remarriage," 104. The same understanding of Matt. 19:9 (the exception clause applies to "whoever divorces" but not to "and marries another") is supported by Andrew Cornes, *Divorce and Remarriage: Biblical Principle and Pastoral Practice*, 2nd ed. (Fearn, Ross-shire, Scotland: Mentor, 2002), 216–19.

marries another," then the verse says, "Whoever divorces his wife, except for sexual immorality, . . . commits adultery." But this is not true, because divorce itself does not constitute adultery. Some people will divorce and not have sex with or marry anybody else. In order to answer such an objection, Heth claims that "divorce is tantamount to committing adultery,"[76] and he appeals to Matthew 5:27–32, but there Jesus does not say that divorce *is* adultery but that someone who wrongly divorces his wife "makes her commit adultery." Nowhere does the Bible say that divorce itself is adultery.

A different explanation of "except for sexual immorality" in Matthew 19:9 is sometimes given by those who support the "no remarriage" position. They argue that *porneia*, as used in Matthew 19:9, does not refer to adultery committed by a married woman but to *fornication by an engaged woman* that is discovered prior to her marriage.[77]

I agree that *porneia*, which refers to a wide range of unlawful sexual activity, was sometimes used to refer to sexual intercourse prior to marriage (see John 8:41). But it was also used to refer to other kinds of sexual immorality, such as incest (1 Cor. 5:1) and adultery (Rev. 17:2; and, from both Jewish and Christian literature near the time of the New Testament, see Sirach 23:23; *Shepherd of Hermas*, Mandate 4.1.5). The most decisive argument against this

76. Heth, "Divorce, but No Remarriage," 104.
77. Heth mentions this view as a "good possibility"; "Divorce, but No Remarriage," 126n66. Piper also favors this interpretation in his "Position Paper," sect. 11.

view is the context of Matthew 19:9, for when the conversation begins, the Pharisees do not ask Jesus about divorce during a betrothal (or engagement) period, but about divorces in general: "And Pharisees came up to him and tested him by asking, 'Is it lawful to divorce one's wife for any cause?'" (Matt. 19:3). Nothing in the context would support limiting the discussion to fornication discovered during the engagement period, nor can it be supported by the common uses of *porneia*, for it refers to a wide variety of sexually immoral acts.

Heth also appeals to Mark 10:11–12 and Luke 16:18,[78] which do not include the exception clause found in Matthew 5:32 and 19:9. I agree that these passages in Mark and Luke do not include an exception for sexual immorality, and if we did not have the verses in Matthew, we might conclude that Jesus did not allow any grounds for divorce. But we do have the verses in Matthew, and they explicitly allow for divorce in the case of sexual immorality. A reasonable explanation is that Mark and Luke did not include Jesus's statement of this exception because there was no dispute about it and everyone agreed that it was a legitimate ground for divorce.

Another argument Heth uses is that "when Paul does specifically discuss the 'right' to remarry he always mentions the matter of the death of one of the spouses in the same context (1 Cor. 7:39; see also Rom. 7:2–3)."[79] But in

---

78. Heth, "Divorce, but No Remarriage," 107–8.
79. Heth, "Divorce, but No Remarriage," 109.

these statements Paul is talking about marriage in general, and the topic of divorce is not in view in either context, so his failure to mention any grounds for divorce in these passages is not a decisive argument.

It is important to note that, in order to be consistent, Heth argues that remarriage is never allowed, not even when the other spouse has married someone else. What is the abandoned spouse to do in such a case? Heth says the abandoned spouse has to remain single for the rest of his or her life:

> If Jesus calls remarriage adultery, and if reconciliation is seemingly impossible, then the path of God's highest blessing must lie in the direction of pursuing a single life.[80]

I appreciate that this is consistent with Heth's understanding of Scripture in his chapter, but it will strike many interpreters as unreasonable. For example, if James and Susan are married, and if James divorces Susan and marries Alice, he is no longer married to Susan. Therefore, Susan is no longer married, but is single (in fact, Heth says she should pursue a "single life"). And if she is single, then there is no reason why she could not marry someone else.

There is another reason why I am not persuaded by the "no remarriage" view, and that is the argument that this position is so unlike the emphasis of the entire New Testament on the healing and restoration of those who have

---

80. Heth, "Divorce, but No Remarriage," 115.

been hurt by the effects of sin and evil in the world. Jesus frequently healed all who were brought to him with any affliction, as we see in verses such as this:

> That evening they brought to him many who were oppressed by demons, and he cast out the spirits with a word and *healed all who were sick*. (Matt. 8:16)

He also said:

> The thief comes only to steal and kill and destroy. I came that they may have life and have it abundantly. (John 10:10)

And the Old Testament said:

> No good thing does he withhold
>   from those who walk uprightly. (Ps. 84:11)

Also, the Bible views marriage as a *blessing* from God, something good and wonderful for us to enjoy during this lifetime (see Gen. 1:31; Prov. 18:22). And marriage presents to the world a beautiful picture of the relationship between Christ and the church (see Eph. 5:31–32).

Therefore, it just does not seem to me to be consistent with the way God acts with his children in the new covenant age to say, for those who have already suffered greatly because a spouse has abandoned them or has committed adultery with someone else, and have suffered even more when that spouse married another person, and who still long to be married, that God would require these suffering victims, *who are no longer married to anyone*, to avoid marrying again for their entire lifetimes. For those who long to marry again, such a prohibition would prolong their hardship and suffering, and it would do so unnecessarily. I simply do not believe that God acts this way with his children in this age.

I recognize that this is a "big-picture" argument that depends on how one sees the New Testament (or the entire Bible) as a whole. I am aware of many passages that speak of the blessings that come to those who endure suffering in this life, and I am sure that those who disagree with me on this topic could quote those passages back to me, and could also quote 1 Corinthians 7 on the value of singleness (for those who are called to such a life and have a gift of celibacy). I realize that in the nature of the Christian life, we will all experience some measure of suffering in this lifetime, for some suffering cannot be avoided. But being prohibited from marriage for the rest of one's lifetime, even for those who do not have the gift of celibacy and who long to be married, is a kind of suffering that *can* be avoided if churches will allow them to remarry. Jesus tells us to pray, "Deliver us from evil" (Matt. 6:13), and surely we should pray that those who have been victims of unwanted divorces would be delivered from their suffering at least to the extent that new marriages would bring healing and blessing to their lives.

Significantly, as I mentioned above, Heth himself later changed his position in a 2002 article entitled "Jesus on

Divorce: How My Mind Has Changed."[81] He wrote, "It seems most probable that the exception clause in Matthew points to divorce with just cause, a valid divorce that would permit remarriage, and Jesus limits that just cause to *porneia*."[82]

Heth also now thinks that 1 Corinthians 7:15 ("But if the unbelieving partner separates, let it be so. In such cases the brother or sister is not enslaved") allows for divorce and remarriage in the case of irreconcilable desertion. He says he was persuaded by Craig Keener's argument that in this verse Paul "distinctly frees the innocent party to remarry" and that "if Paul meant that remarriage was not permitted, he said precisely the opposite of what he meant."[83]

H. PRACTICAL COUNSEL REGARDING PEOPLE WHO HAVE EXPERIENCED PAINFUL DIVORCES

Probably every church today has people who have experienced painful divorces—perhaps some children who still are deeply grieved because their mothers and fathers dissolved their marriages many years ago, or perhaps adults who did not want a divorce at all but whose spouses filed for divorce anyway. As the Wallerstein study mentioned earlier in this book demonstrated, such people can experience deep pain

81. Heth, "Jesus on Divorce: How My Mind Has Changed," 4–29.

82. Heth, "Jesus on Divorce: How My Mind Has Changed," 20.

83. Heth, "Jesus on Divorce: How My Mind Has Changed," 13, quoting Craig Keener, *And Marries Another: Divorce and Remarriage in the Teaching of the New Testament* (Peabody, MA: Hendrickson, 1991), 61.

and sorrow, and the feeling of being deserted and betrayed, many years later—though they will seldom mention it to anyone.

It is important that pastors and other church members be aware that such situations are not uncommon today. At some place and time in the life of the church, it is important to provide a setting in which people feel sufficiently safe to discuss these feelings and then have opportunity to pray with one or two others at some length, until the Holy Spirit gives them the ability to genuinely forgive the ones who caused their hurt and brings genuine comfort and peace to the grieving individuals' hearts and minds.

Christians who have been through divorces also have a wonderful encouragement to realize that Jesus understands our sufferings and is willing to walk beside us in them:

> For we do not have a high priest who is unable to sympathize with our weaknesses, but one who in every respect has been tempted as we are, yet without sin. Let us then with confidence draw near to the throne of grace, that we may receive mercy and find grace to help in time of need. (Heb. 4:15–16)

Although Jesus was never married, and so he never experienced divorce specifically, he certainly knew what it was to be betrayed and abandoned by friends who were close to him, particularly Judas, who had been with him for three remarkable years (see Matt. 26:14, 25, 47; see also v. 56: "all the disciples left him and fled"). Christians can pray directly to Jesus, knowing that he understands desertion more deeply than any human friend ever will.

It is also important for Christians who have experienced divorces not to let the rest of their lives be ruled by this pain from the past. For children who have suffered deeply from divorces, Peter's words have special relevance, showing that Christ's sacrifice purchased freedom for us even from any wrongful patterns of life that we experienced from our parents:

> You were *ransomed from the futile ways inherited from your forefathers*, not with perishable things such as silver or gold, but with the precious blood of Christ, like that of a lamb without blemish or spot. (1 Pet. 1:18–19)

And for adults who have been abandoned by a previous wife or husband, the promise of God's comfort in 2 Corinthians should also bring great encouragement:

> Blessed be the God and Father of our Lord Jesus Christ, the Father of mercies and God of all comfort, who comforts us in all our affliction, so that we may be able to comfort those who are in any affliction, with the comfort with which we ourselves are comforted by God. For as we share abundantly in Christ's sufferings, so through Christ we share abundantly in comfort too. (2 Cor. 1:3–5)

Finally, it is important for churches to establish programs or ministry practices that teach about and encourage strong marriages, and that also will provide counseling and help for couples who are going through difficult times in their marriages.[84]

And for every married person reading this book, even those who wrongfully were divorced in the past and have now married someone else, God's purpose for you from this point onward is to ask him for forgiveness for wrongs done in the past and then to seek God's blessing *on your present marriage*. He does not want you now to get another divorce, but to stay married. Therefore, no matter what circumstances led up to this present marriage, if you are married, *you are now married to the right person*, and God wants you to make that marriage a good one for the rest of your life.

I. APPENDIX: THE TRANSLATION OF MALACHI 2:16

There are three main translation options for Malachi 2:16:

1. Several translations have the Lord saying, "I hate divorce," as in the NASB:

> "For *I hate divorce*," says the LORD, the God of Israel, "and him who covers his garment with wrong," says the LORD of hosts. "So take heed to your spirit, that you do not deal treacherously." (Mal. 2:16, NASB)

The RSV, NRSV, NIV 1984, NLT, and NET also have the Lord saying, "I hate divorce."

---

84. FamilyLife, a Christian ministry that until 2017 was led by my longtime friend Dennis Rainey, is an outstanding, biblically sound organization that has a variety of excellent programs to encourage and strengthen marriages. See http://www.familylife.com. (Margaret and I were previously members of the Speaker Team for FamilyLife marriage conferences.)

2. Other translations, such as the NIV 2011, understand the subject of "hates" to be the husband, and they translate this sentence this way:

"*The man who hates and divorces his wife*," says the LORD, the God of Israel, "does violence to the one he should protect," says the LORD Almighty. (Mal. 2:16, NIV)

The ESV translation is similar, but it understands "hates" to mean failing to love one's wife:

For *the man who does not love his wife but divorces her*, says the LORD, the God of Israel, covers his garment with violence, says the LORD of hosts. (Mal. 2:16, ESV)

The Christian Standard Bible is also similar: "'If he hates and divorces *his wife*,' says the LORD God of Israel, 'he covers his garment with injustice,' says the LORD of Armies" (Mal. 2:16, CSB).

3. A third alternative is to translate the verb as "he hates," but to understand "the Lord" to be the subject, not the husband. This is the alternative translation found in the marginal note of the ESV:

Or "The LORD, the God of Israel, says that *he hates divorce*." (Mal. 2:16, ESV mg.)

The NKJV also translates it this way: "For the LORD God of Israel says that *He hates divorce*." The KJV is similar: "For the LORD, the God of Israel, saith that he hateth putting away: for *one* covereth violence with his garment, saith the Lord of hosts."

Is there a best solution among these three options? The Hebrew of this verse is notoriously difficult to understand. No solution is without difficulties. Here are the three main solutions, with the arguments in favor of each:

1. Several translations have God saying, "I hate divorce" (NASB, RSV, NRSV, NET, NIV 1984, and NLT). To render the Hebrew text this way, the translators have to understand the verb *sānē'* as a participle, "hating" (ordinarily this would be spelled *sonē'*), and assume that the pronoun "I" is understood, giving the sense, "For I hate [am hating] divorce, says the Lord" (Zech. 9:12 is cited as a parallel in Hebrew). On this view, as well as view 3, some slight change has to be made to the third-person singular verb *wekissāh*, "and he covers," in the next clause, altering it to say something like "and the one who covers" or "and covering."

2. The ESV understands the first clause in a sense similar to the Septuagint, taking the Hebrew to represent an "if-then" statement, because the first word (Hebrew, *kî*) can mean either "for" or "if." This gives the sense, "If he [that is, a man] hates and divorces, says the Lord God of Israel, he covers his garment with violence." Reasons in support of this sense are: (1) It understands the subject of "hates" as a divorcing husband, which is consistent with the use of "hate" in marriage contexts elsewhere,

where the hatred in question is invariably the husband's (Gen. 29:31; Deut. 21:15–17; 22:13, 16; 24:3; Judg. 15:2; Prov. 30:23). In some of these cases, "hate" has the sense "cease to love," and this is how the ESV translates the verb. (2) This translation requires no change of the Hebrew text. (3) The alternative translations "I hate divorce" or "the Lord . . . says that he hates divorce" sound like a complete condemnation of divorce, but such a blanket condemnation of divorce in Malachi 2:16 would contradict the qualified permission, at least as a response to sexuality infidelity, that is implied by Deuteronomy 22:19, 29; 24:1–4; Jeremiah 3 (God's figurative divorce of Israel); Matthew 5:32; 19:8–9; and 1 Corinthians 7:15. (4) The subject of the second verb must be a sinful human being, for it cannot mean, "For the Lord says that he hates divorce *and he covers his garment with violence.*" Therefore, other translations have to change the finite third-person verb "and he covers" (Hebrew, *wekissāh*) to a participle, giving the sense "and *covering* one's garment with violence."

3. An ESV footnote gives this alternative sense: "The Lord, the God of Israel, says that he hates divorce, and him who covers . . ." Supporting reasons are: (1) "The Lord" is the only person explicitly named in the verse, and it is natural to understand him as the one about whom the verse says, "he hates." (2) Several other examples of this exact grammatical construction in Hebrew (perfect verb plus infinitive with no conjunction or preposition between

them) show that the infinitive should be taken as the direct object of the first verb, giving the sense, "he hates [perfect verb] divorce [infinitive]" (cf. Num. 10:31; Deut. 2:7; Pss. 77:10 [English v. 9]; 139:2; Isa. 56:11). But there are no examples of this combination in the Hebrew Old Testament that would support the sense of "and" in "he hates *and* divorces." What is needed for view 2 is some example of a finite verb X (such as "he hates") followed immediately by an infinitive Y (such as "divorce") where it means "X and Y," but no examples have been found. (3) All of the other 60 Old Testament instances of a finite form of this same verb *sānē'* ("hate") have an object expressed (the person or thing hated). Therefore, this verb must require a direct object here as well, and this supports the sense "he hates divorce" (with "divorce" as the direct object), but not the sense "he hates and divorces" (with no expressed object for "hate"). (4) In other contexts that mention sin, where "the Lord" is mentioned along with the word *hates* (Hebrew, *sānē'*), the Lord is often the subject (e.g., Isa. 1:14; 61:8; Jer. 44:4; Zech. 8:17; Mal. 1:3). (5) This verse then gives a clear reason for Malachi 2:15: Let no one be faithless to his wife (v. 15) *for* (Hebrew, *kî*) the Lord hates divorce (v. 16).

The decision is not an easy one, but the translation of the ESV footnote (and KJV and NKJV), represented by view 3, seems somewhat preferable to me for the reasons given above: "The LORD, the God of Israel, says that he hates divorce."

In any case, the Bible's teaching on divorce is not changed by any of these translations, because all of them signify that divorce for reasons not specified elsewhere in Scripture is condemned by the Lord as a serious sin. On interpretations 1 and 3, what the Lord "hates" is probably only the kind of "faithless" sending away of one's wife mentioned in the context (see vv. 13, 15); or the verse may be speaking to God's hatred of the destructiveness and pain that is always involved with divorce.

FURTHER RESOURCES

QUESTIONS FOR PERSONAL APPLICATION

1. Were you surprised by the information in this book about how many marriages are happy and about how few Christian marriages end in divorce? What was the source of your previous ideas regarding how many marriages succeed?

2. Were you surprised to read about the long-term consequences of divorce? How did this material affect your thinking about divorce?

3. After reading the discussion in this book, how many legitimate grounds do you think there are for divorce, according to the New Testament? In such cases, do you think that remarriage to another person is morally acceptable?

4. What character traits would be most helpful in protecting a marriage so that it does not end in divorce? Which ones would be most important in dealing with the consequences of an unwanted divorce?

5. Read Exodus 20:17. Do you ever "covet your neighbor's wife" (or husband)? Are you willing right now to bring that desire into the presence of God, ask his forgiveness, and ask for his help in changing that desire in your heart into a positive desire for your own wife or husband?

6. If you are married, what are some practical things you can do now to strengthen your marriage and help to protect it from ending in divorce?

BIBLIOGRAPHY

Sections in Christian Ethics Texts

Clark, David K., and Robert V. Rakestraw, eds. *Readings in Christian Ethics*. 2 vols. Grand Rapids, MI: Baker, 1994, 2:225–60.

Davis, John Jefferson. *Evangelical Ethics: Issues Facing the Church Today*. 4th ed. Phillipsburg, NJ: P&R, 2015, 90–105.

Feinberg, John S., and Paul D. Feinberg. *Ethics for a Brave New World*. 2nd ed. Wheaton, IL: Crossway, 2010, 583–633.

Frame, John M. *The Doctrine of the Christian Life: A Theology of Lordship*. Phillipsburg, NJ: P&R, 2008, 769–81.

Geisler, Norman L. *Christian Ethics: Contemporary Issues and Options*. 2nd ed. Grand Rapids, MI: Baker, 2010, 303–13.

Gushee, David P., and Glen H. Stassen. *Kingdom Ethics: Following Jesus in Contemporary Context*. 2nd ed. Grand Rapids, MI: Eerdmans, 2016, 270–87.

Hays, Richard B. *The Moral Vision of the New Testament: Community, Cross, New Creation: A Contemporary Introduction to New Testament Ethics*. San Francisco: HarperSanFrancisco, 1996, 347–78.

Jones, David Clyde. *Biblical Christian Ethics*. Grand Rapids, MI: Baker, 1994, 177–204.

Kaiser, Walter C., Jr. *What Does the Lord Require? A Guide for Preaching and Teaching Biblical Ethics*. Grand Rapids, MI: Baker, 2009, 91–104.

McQuilkin, Robertson, and Paul Copan. *An Introduction to Biblical Ethics: Walking in the Way of Wisdom*. 3rd ed. Downers Grove, IL: InterVarsity Press, 2014, 241–48.

Other Works

Adams, Jay E. *Marriage, Divorce, and Remarriage in the Bible*. Grand Rapids, MI: Zondervan, 1980.

Atkinson, D. J. "Remarriage." In *New Dictionary of Christian Ethics and Pastoral Theology*, edited by David J. Atkinson and David H. Field, 729–30. Leicester, UK: Inter-Varsity, and Downers Grove, IL: InterVarsity Press, 1995.

Cornes, Andrew. *Divorce and Remarriage: Biblical Principle and Pastoral Practice*. 2nd ed. Fearn, Ross-shire, Scotland: Mentor, 2002.

Feldhahn, Shaunti. *The Good News about Marriage: Debunking Discouraging Myths about Marriage and Divorce*. Colorado Springs: Multnomah, 2014.

Hawthorne, Gerald F. "Marriage and Divorce, Adultery and Incest." In *Dictionary of Paul and His Letters*, edited by Gerald F. Hawthorne, Ralph P. Martin, and Daniel G. Reid, 594–600. Downers Grove, IL: InterVarsity Press, 1993.

Heth, William A., and Gordon J. Wenham. *Jesus and Divorce: The Problem with the Evangelical Consensus*. Nashville: Thomas Nelson, 1984.

House, H. Wayne, ed. *Divorce and Remarriage: Four Christian Views*. Downers Grove, IL: InterVarsity Press, 1990.

Instone-Brewer, David. *Divorce and Remarriage in the Bible: The Social and Literary Context*. Grand Rapids, MI: Eerdmans, 2002.

———. *Divorce and Remarriage in the Church: Biblical Solutions for Pastoral Realities*. Downers Grove, IL: InterVarsity Press, 2003.

Keener, Craig S. *And Marries Another: Divorce and Remarriage in the Teaching of the New Testament*. Peabody, MA: Hendrickson, 1991.

Köstenberger, Andreas J., with David W. Jones. *God, Marriage, and Family: Rebuilding the Biblical Foundation*. 2nd ed. Wheaton, IL: Crossway, 2010, 223–38, 275–88, 363–69, 373–77.

Laney, J. Carl. *The Divorce Myth: A Biblical Examination of Divorce and Remarriage*. Minneapolis: Bethany House, 1981.

MacArthur, John. *The Divorce Dilemma: God's Last Word on Lasting Commitment*. Family Focal Point. Leominster, England: Day One, 2009.

Moles, Chris. *The Heart of Domestic Abuse: Gospel Solutions for Men Who Use Control and Violence in the Home*. Bemidji, MN: Focus, 2015.

Murray, John. *Divorce*. Philadelphia: Presbyterian & Reformed, 1961.

Newheiser, Jim. *Marriage, Divorce, and Remarriage: Critical Questions and Answers*. Phillipsburg, NJ: P&R, 2017.

Roberts, Barbara. *Not under Bondage: Biblical Divorce for Abuse, Adultery and Desertion*. N.p.: Maschil Press, 2008.

Small, Dwight Hervey. *Remarriage and God's Renewing Grace: A Positive Biblical Ethic for Divorced Christians.* Grand Rapids, MI: Baker, 1986.

Storms, Sam. "What Did Jesus Teach about Divorce and Remarriage? What Did Paul Teach about Divorce and Remarriage?" In *Tough Topics 2: Biblical Answers to 25 Challenging Questions*, 209–35. Fearn, Ross-shire, Scotland: Christian Focus, 2015.

Strauss, Mark L., ed. *Remarriage after Divorce in Today's Church: Three Views.* Counterpoints. Grand Rapids, MI: Zondervan, 2006.

Tracy, Steven R. *Mending the Soul: Understanding and Healing Abuse.* Grand Rapids, MI: Zondervan, 2005.

Wallerstein, Judith S., Julia Lewis, and Sandra Blakeslee. *The Unexpected Legacy of Divorce: A 25 Year Landmark Study.* New York: Hyperion, 2000.

Wallerstein, Judith S., and Sandra Blakeslee. *Second Chances: Men, Women, and Children a Decade after Divorce.* New York: Ticknor & Fields, 1989.

Wenham, Gordon J. "Divorce." In *New Dictionary of Christian Ethics and Pastoral Theology*, 315–17.

———. *Jesus, Divorce, and Remarriage.* Bellingham, WA: Lexham, 2019.

Wenham, Gordon J., and William A. Heth. *Jesus and Divorce: Towards an Evangelical Understanding of New Testament Teaching.* 2nd ed. Carlisle, UK: Paternoster, 2002.

SCRIPTURE MEMORY PASSAGE

Matthew 19:9: And I say to you: whoever divorces his wife, except for sexual immorality, and marries another, commits adultery.

HYMN

"Like a River Glorious"

Like a river glorious is God's perfect peace,
Over all victorious in its bright increase;
Perfect, yet it floweth fuller ev'ry day,
Perfect, yet it groweth deeper all the way.

Refrain:
Stayed upon Jehovah,
Hearts are fully blest
Finding, as He promised,
Perfect peace and rest.

Hidden in the hollow of His blessed hand,
Never foe can follow, never traitor stand;
Not a surge of worry, not a shade of care,
Not a blast of hurry touch the spirit there.

Ev'ry joy or trial falleth from above,
Traced upon our dial by the Sun of Love;
We may trust Him fully all for us to do—
They who trust Him wholly, find Him wholly true.

Frances R. Havergal, 1836–1879

ALTERNATIVE HYMN
"I Need Thee Every Hour"

I need Thee ev'ry hour,
Most gracious Lord;
No tender voice like Thine
Can peace afford.

Refrain:
I need Thee, O I need Thee,
Ev'ry hour I need Thee!
O bless me now, my Savior
I come to Thee!

I need Thee ev'ry hour,
Stay Thou nearby;
Temptations lose their pow'r
When Thou art nigh.

I need Thee ev'ry hour,
In joy or pain;
Come quickly and abide,
Or life is vain.

I need Thee ev'ry hour,
Most Holy One;
O make me Thine indeed,
Thou blessed Son!

Annie S. Hawks, 1835–1918

Scripture Versions Cited

General Index

Scripture Index

Also Available from Wayne Grudem

In this comprehensive volume on Christian ethics, best-selling author Wayne Grudem explains in detail what the whole Bible says about living as a Christian.

"Insightful, encyclopedic, biblical, and distinctively evangelical, this book from Wayne Grudem is a massive contribution to Christian ethics."
R. ALBERT MOHLER JR.

For more information, visit **crossway.org**.

Accessible Booklets Answering Complex Ethical Questions

What the Bible Says about

HOW TO KNOW GOD'S WILL

Wayne Grudem

What the Bible Says about

ABORTION, EUTHANASIA, AND END-OF-LIFE MEDICAL DECISIONS

Wayne Grudem

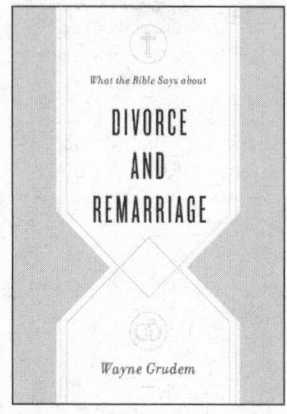

What the Bible Says about

DIVORCE AND REMARRIAGE

Wayne Grudem

What the Bible Says about

BIRTH CONTROL, INFERTILITY, REPRODUCTIVE TECHNOLOGY, AND ADOPTION

Wayne Grudem